The Athlete Burnout Questionnaire Manual

The Athlete Burnout Questionnaire Manual

Thomas D. Raedeke
East Carolina University

Alan L. Smith
Purdue University

Dedication

To my sons, Tyler and Sean, who give me perspective
and keep me balanced
T.D.R.

To Mom, Dad, Jennifer, and Cody
A.L.S.

Copyright © 2009 by West Virginia University

All rights reserved.

Reproduction or use of any portion of this publication by any mechanical, electronic, or other means is prohibited without written permission of the publisher.

Library of Congress Card Catalog Number: 2008933800

ISBN 13: 978-1-885693-88-4

Production Editor: Valerie Gittings
Cover Design: Scott Lohr, 40 West Studios
Typesetter: Jamie Merlavage
Copyeditor: Matthew Brann
Proofreader: Erica Reib
Printed by: Data Reproductions

10 9 8 7 6 5 4 3 2 1

Fitness Information Technology
A Division of the International Center for Performance Excellence
West Virginia University
262 Coliseum, WVU-PE
PO Box 6116
Morgantown, WV 26506-6116
800.477.4348 (toll free)
304.293.6888 (phone)
304.293.6658 (fax)
Email: icpe@mail.wvu.edu
Website: www.fitinfotech.com

About the Sport and Exercise Psychology Test Clearinghouse

This test manual is the fourth in our Sport and Exercise Psychology Test Clearinghouse. For the first time ever, sport psychology researchers have produced comprehensive manuals to some of the most popular assessment tools on the market. Each manual in the Clearinghouse focuses on a specific conceptual area of sport psychology research and practice, and it provides students and researchers with literature background and information pertaining to the psychometric development of each test.

I am excited that the fourth book in the series focuses on a very important topic in sport today, namely burnout. The authors of this manual have compiled a wealth of useful information related to the assessment of burnout and the development of this instrument. As Editor-in-Chief of the Clearinghouse, I have the privilege of reviewing each book in the library, as well as facilitating an external, peer review of the work. I can assure you that the product you have purchased is one of good academic quality, and I hope it will make your work in the area of sport burnout more efficient and productive.

Best of luck in your research and applied endeavors!

Sam Zizi
Editor-in-Chief
Sport and Exercise Psychology Test Clearinghouse

Sam Zizzi, EdD, is an associate professor at West Virginia University, where he teaches courses in sport and exercise psychology, statistics, and research methods and also serves as a statistical consultant to several graduate programs, including athletic training and counseling psychology. On the applied side, he supervises graduate students, works with WVU athletes on performance enhancement, and is a Certified

Consultant (AASP) and member of the US Olympic Committee's Sport Psychology Registry. In addition, he coordinates the exercise adherence and weight loss programs run through the university for community members. When not working on academic pursuits, Sam prefers to roam the planet with friends and family. He can usually be found with his beautiful wife, Elizabeth, and baby daughter, Adelina, engaging in physical activities including swimming, basketball, racquetball, rollerblading, and raftball. He also enjoys playing guitar for his two favorite ladies and spending quality time outdoors with his smiling puppy, Lucy.

Acknowledgments

We have had the good fortune of being guided by strong mentors and surrounded by exceptional colleagues and students as we have progressed through our careers. We thank these individuals for the important contributions they have made to our views on sport psychology and to our professional development. In particular, we wish to thank those who have collaborated with us in our scholarship on burnout and those who have made efforts to assess the integrity of the Athlete Burnout Questionnaire (ABQ). This group includes Jennifer Black, Scott Cresswell, Robert Eklund, Jennifer Glass, Tracy Granzyk, Kimberly Hurley, Ken Hodge, Göran Kenttä, Nicolas Lemyre, Chris Lonsdale, Kevin Lunney, Sarah Ullrich-French, Kirk Venables, Anne Warren, Maureen Weiss, and many others. We would also like to thank Val Gittings, Andrew Ostrow, and Sam Zizzi, key members of the Fitness Information Technology team, who supported our efforts in producing this manual. Finally, we would like to thank the athletes and coaches who have supported our work on the ABQ by giving generously of their time and energy.

Responsibilities of the Purchaser of the Athlete Burnout Questionnaire

Part 1: User's Scientific Responsibilities

1. I will carefully read this test manual before administering the Athlete Burnout Questionnaire (ABQ).

2. I will have had sufficient training using the ABQ prior to administering this measure (i.e. If a professional, I am in possession of a master's degree or doctorate in sport psychology or a related discipline; If a student, I am working under the supervision of a professional with sufficient training in psychometrics).

3. I have read and will adhere to the ethical principles outlined in the American Psychological Association's *Ethical Principles of Psychologists and Code of Conduct* (APA, 2002), especially section 8 ("Research and Publication") and section 9 ("Assessment"). I have also reviewed *Standards for Educational and Psychological Testing* (AERA, 1999).

4. When administering the ABQ, I will adhere to the standards required for the protection of human subjects as specified by APA and my institution's human subjects/ethics review boards. These standards include, but are not limited to:

    - the protection of the confidentiality of participants,
    - the rights of participants to receive information on the purposes of the athlete burnout questionnaire,
    - the potential uses of the test results, and
    - the methods of test score feedback to individual test participants.

5. Before making modifications to the ABQ, I will carefully review the test manual to determine the appropriateness of the modification(s).

6. I understand that the scoring profiles provided in the test manual may not be applicable to modified or translated versions of the ABQ.

Part 2: User's Responsibilities to FIT

1. I understand that I am required to contact Fitness Information Technology (FIT) at fitcustomerservice@mail.wvu.edu for permission to translate the ABQ into another language. I will carefully review *The Athlete Burnout Questionnaire Manual* and consider relevant cultural matters to ensure that an appropriate translation of the ABQ is produced.

2. I understand that, while copyright of the ABQ test materials and products is held by the test authors, the test authors have granted the publisher, Fitness Information Technology, the right to distribute and sell the ABQ test materials and products on a worldwide basis.

3. I understand that it is a violation of copyright law if I distribute, sell, or license to third parties copies of the ABQ test materials and products without first obtaining written permission from Fitness Information Technology.

Table of Contents

Foreword xiii

Preface xv

Chapter 1: Administering the Athlete Burnout Questionnaire 1

   Item and Response Format of the ABQ

   Administering the ABQ

   Appropriate ABQ Respondent Samples

Chapter 2: The Burnout Construct 7

   The Origins of the Burnout Construct

   Conceptual Ambiguity Surrounding Burnout

   Burnout as a Syndrome

   The Foundation of the ABQ: Defining Athlete Burnout

   Debated Issues in Conceptualizing Burnout

   Preliminary Item Development

Chapter 3: Within-Network Validation 21

   Evaluation of a Preliminary Version of the ABQ

   Evaluation of the Factor Structure of a Revised ABQ

   Reliability and Scale Intercorrelations

   Multitrait-Multimethod Evaluation of the ABQ

Chapter 4: Between-Network Validation 33

Chapter 5: ABQ Score Profiles 45

References 57

Appendix A: The Athlete Burnout Questionnaire 63

Appendix B: Scoring of the Athlete Burnout Questionnaire 65

About the Authors 67

Foreword

Athlete burnout has long been an area of interest and speculation among sport aficionados and sport scientists alike. Many people believed that the term "burnout" captured the essence of unsettling difficulties observed among athletes relative to performance, their commitment to sport, and in their personal lives. Precisely what this widely used term actually meant was nowhere near as clear as the building consensus that something needed to be done in this area of growing disquiet in the sporting world, and there was no shortage of commentary (albeit little data) on that account in the extant literature.

Two fundamental issues had to be resolved before any progress could be made in building an empirical basis to address this problem. First, as ably discussed in this manual, the term "burnout" was widely employed, but unfortunately, the intended meaning varied widely. A need existed for a precise conceptualization of the burnout construct to replace the widespread "everyone knows what it is" usage evident across the many colloquial and scientific commentaries on the subject. Second, once precisely conceptualized, a valid and reliable measurement tool was required to operationalize the construct. Raedeke and Smith addressed both of these issues in developing the Athlete Burnout Questionnaire (ABQ). They grounded their conceptualization of athlete burnout in Maslach's (1982) well-established and well-formalized burnout syndrome and produced a reliable and valid measure of the construct. The ABQ, as such, represents the resolution of two fundamental barriers to the growth of scientific knowledge on athlete burnout and a major accomplishment in terms of providing a basis for growth of a coherent body of research in the area.

The study of athlete burnout has expanded dramatically over the last decade and become a vibrant area of scholarly inquiry, even to the extent that an entire special issue on athlete burnout was recently published by the *International Journal of Sport Psychology*. In good measure, the ABQ has provided an important impetus for this growth and focused researchers' attention onto the burnout syndrome as the epicenter of study. Raedeke and Smith are congratulated on providing this platform to expand knowledge in the area. The *ABQ Manual* further advances this cause by providing a succinct but informative resource outlining the conceptual basis of the athlete burnout syndrome and its measurement. I anticipate that it will serve researchers studying this unfortunate experiential syndrome well and further expand the community of researchers studying in the area.

Robert C. Eklund, PhD, FACSM

Florida State University

Preface

Developing a questionnaire to assess burnout is a complex and challenging task. The overall aim of this manual is to delineate the process used in developing the Athlete Burnout Questionnaire (ABQ), as well as provide ABQ users with information on the meaning of scores derived from this measure. To set the foundation for discussing ABQ development efforts, we describe the validation process and give an overview of how each chapter in this manual addresses different facets of that process.

Validity is widely considered the most fundamental issue in developing, evaluating, and using a measure (AERA, 1999; Rowe & Mahar, 2006), with the central concern being the accuracy of inferences about the construct that are derived from the measurement tool. How well do scores derived from the measurement tool reflect the construct or characteristic they are designed to represent? Over the past few decades, views on validity have changed substantially. Historically, validity was viewed as a property of the measure itself (i.e., Is the questionnaire valid?). This is no longer the case, as validity now centers on evaluating inferences about a construct that are made from a measure. Thus, validity is about the meaning and interpretation of scores derived from questionnaire items. Specifically, validity is the degree to which evidence and theory support the intended meaning and interpretation of scores derived from a questionnaire about a construct. The validation process involves accumulating evidence to establish a strong scientific basis to support intended score interpretation (AERA, 1999; Messick, 1995; Zumbo, 2005).

Aligned with contemporary views on validity, Chapter 1 includes the ABQ, along with the guidelines for administering and scoring it. Questionnaire development and the validation process are guided by the intended inferences to be made from scores derived from that measure and the context and populations for which a measure is intended to be used. Consequently, part of the validation process involves describing test specifications (e.g., item and response format, administration and scoring procedures), as well as intended uses of the scale.

In the past, psychometricians described several different types of validity (e.g., content, criterion [predictive and concurrent], and construct [convergent and divergent]). Contemporary views forward validity as a unified concept under the auspices of construct validity. Construct validity is defined as the extent to which scores derived from a measure assess the construct they are designed to measure, rather than some other construct. The validity of score interpretation is specific to the population being assessed and the setting in which assessment occurs. Rather than investigating different types of validity, a more contemporary approach is to evaluate various sources of evidence that provide insights on inferences made about a construct from a measure (AERA, 1999; Marsh, 1998; Rowe & Mahar, 2006).

Evaluating construct validity is an ongoing process that occurs in multiple stages. Although authors use varying terms to describe the various types of evidence associated with construct validity, there is some uniformity across authors regarding the processes and types of evidence gathered to evaluate the accuracy of inferences about a construct that are based on responses to questionnaire items (AERA, 1999; Clark & Watson, 1995; Marsh, 1998; Rowe & Mahar, 2006).

The first stage in the scale development process is called the definitional stage (Rowe & Mahar, 2006) and involves substantive validity evidence (Clark & Watson, 1995). This source of evidence is similar to what has been traditionally called content or logical validity. At this stage, the researcher defines the conceptual underpinnings of the construct and develops an item pool to measure the construct. Two central issues at this point of the validation process involve (a) using theory and empirical evidence to provide the conceptual foundation for the measure and (b) developing an item pool that is representative and adequately reflects the breadth of the construct being assessed. Aligned with this stage of questionnaire development, Chapter 2 covers the conceptual underpinnings of the ABQ. Within this chapter, we provide an overview of the burnout construct and the operational definition used to guide item development. We also describe how the preliminary item pool was developed.

The second source of validity evidence is called structural validity (Clark & Watson, 1995) or within-network (Marsh, 1998) evidence. This is also called the confirmatory stage of construct validation (Rowe & Mahar, 2006), as it focuses on gathering evidence to evaluate the definition and internal structure of a construct. Investigators evaluate whether the internal structure exhibited by item scores confirms or disconfirms the description of the construct being assessed. Researchers may, for example, test the dimensionality of the construct through factor analysis.

They may also use a multitrait-multimethod approach to evaluate the internal structure. In Chapter 3, we review research using a within-network approach to examining the internal structure of the burnout construct based on the ABQ. This includes factor analysis results examining dimensionality, research evaluating intecorrelations of burnout dimensions, and a multitrait-multimethod matrix approach to evaluating internal structure. Given the central role of reliability in evaluating measurement quality, this chapter also includes a description of both internal consistency and stability of ABQ scores.

Although assessing dimensionality and reliability are important aspects of questionnaire development, they are often viewed as necessary but not sufficient conditions in construct validation efforts. A final source of evidence in the construct validation process involves theory testing (Rowe & Mahar, 2006) and examining the relationship of scores from a target measure with theoretically relevant constructs. This source of evidence is also called between-network (Marsh, 1998) or nomological evidence (Rowe & Mahar, 2006), and involves delineating a hypothesized network of interrelationships between the construct being assessed and other constructs and evaluating whether a predicted pattern of relationships exists. Consequently, the focus of Chapter 4 is to discuss a between-network approach to construct validation by examining the relationship of ABQ scores to theoretically relevant variables stemming from stress, sociological, and motivational perspectives on burnout.

Finally, in Chapter 5, we provide basic descriptive statistical information that can help users interpret the meaning of scores derived from the ABQ. Given that the meaning of scores derived from the ABQ are bound by contextual factors and dependent on the population being assessed, we also provide descriptive information for various subgroups of athletes including female–male, adolescent–college/adult, individual sport–team sport, and training intensive sport–not training intensive sport.

In conclusion, this test manual provides users with information for using the ABQ and evidence on construct validity. However, it is important to note that accumulating validity evidence is an ongoing process. As new knowledge on ABQ score meaning emerges, revisions to the ABQ and the conceptual framework that undergirds it may be needed. Our goal in developing the ABQ and this test manual is to stimulate research on athlete burnout, and we are eager to see how such research evolves. We are optimistic that ultimately this work will lead to preventative strategies and help ensure that athletes have positive competitive sport experiences.

Chapter 1: Administering the Athlete Burnout Questionnaire

This chapter introduces the Athlete Burnout Questionnaire (ABQ), including a description of its subscales, item and response format, and guidelines for administering and scoring the scale. The ABQ was derived from a definition of athlete burnout (Raedeke, 1997; Raedeke & Smith, 2001) that was based on and modified from the predominant conceptualization of burnout employed in the human service and organizational psychology literatures (e.g., Maslach & Goldberg, 1998; Maslach, Jackson, & Leiter, 1996; Maslach, Schaufeli, & Leiter, 2001; Schaufeli, Maslach, & Marek, 1993). Based on this framework, burnout is viewed as an experiential state ranging from low to high levels, rather than a dichotomous state of being burned out or not. Athlete burnout is also viewed as a multidimensional construct consisting of three dimensions: emotional/physical exhaustion, reduced sense of accomplishment, and sport devaluation. Therefore, the ABQ consists of three subscales that capture these burnout dimensions, as defined below.

- *Emotional/physical exhaustion* is characterized by feelings of emotional and physical fatigue stemming from the psychosocial and physical demands associated with training and competing.

- *Reduced sense of accomplishment* is characterized by feelings of inefficacy and a tendency to evaluate oneself negatively in terms of sport performance and accomplishments.

- *Sport devaluation* is defined as a negative, detached attitude toward sport, reflected by lack of concern about sport and performance quality.

Item and Response Format of the ABQ

Based on a multidimensional conceptualization of athlete burnout, the ABQ consists of 15 items in total, with five items tapping each athlete burnout dimension (see Table 1.1). In completing the scale, participants rate how frequently they have experienced the content of each item on a five-point Likert-type scale of: (1) *almost never*, (2) *rarely*, (3) *sometimes*, (4) *frequently*, and (5) *almost always*. Given that athlete burnout is conceptualized as a relatively chronic state, respondents are instructed to complete the ABQ in terms of the frequency of their thoughts and feelings over the entire current season. Some researchers will wish to modify this time frame, depending on features of their research question and methodological design. Also, the word [*sport*] can be replaced with the specific sport of a respondent.

Table 1.1: ABQ Items Organized by Subscale

Item Number	Item Text
Emotional/Physical Exhaustion	
2.	I feel so tired from my training that I have trouble finding energy to do other things
4.	I feel overly tired from my [sport] participation
8.	I feel "wiped out" from [sport]
10.	I feel physically worn out from [sport]
12.	I am exhausted by the mental and physical demands of [sport]
Reduced Sense of Accomplishment	
1.	I'm accomplishing many worthwhile things in [sport]
5.	I am not achieving much in [sport]
7.	I am not performing up to my ability in [sport]
13.	It seems that no matter what I do, I don't perform as well as I should
14.	I feel successful at [sport]
Sport Devaluation	
3.	The effort I spend in [sport] would be better spent doing other things
6.	I don't care as much about my [sport] performance as I used to
9.	I'm not into [sport] like I used to be
11.	I feel less concerned about being successful in [sport] than I used to
15.	I have negative feelings toward [sport]

Notes: Items 1 and 14 are reverse scored. The specific sport of the respondent is inserted where [sport] appears above.

In scoring the ABQ, items from each subscale are summed and divided by five. Thus, three subscale scores are obtained that each range from one to five. Items 1 and 14, both of which are reduced sense of accomplishment items, are reverse scored before computing subscale scores.

Administering the ABQ

The ABQ takes approximately five minutes to complete. Given that athletes (and others that work with them) can be sensitive to the term "burnout" in reference to their athletic endeavors, it is important to minimize response biases when administering the ABQ. Therefore, when administering the ABQ:

- *Avoid Referring to the Term "Burnout."* The term "burnout" is associated with a variety of connotations and meanings. In everyday discourse, burnout is at times viewed in the context of a temporary state of fatigue. At other times, it is viewed more negatively and as a sign of mental weakness or a character flaw of the athlete. Given the varied personal meanings of the term and the potential negative stigma associated with burnout, it is recommended to not use the term when introducing the ABQ. This will help avoid sensitizing participants to the general issue of burnout. Instead, the ABQ can be introduced in general terms, such as a survey to assess sport-related experiences and thoughts/feelings. This is consistent with the items themselves, as they make no explicit reference to "burnout." Aligned with these recommendations, we suggest using a general title such as "Sport Experience Questionnaire" in lieu of "Athlete Burnout Questionnaire" when administering the ABQ. Alternatively, a title can be omitted altogether if the ABQ is administered as part of larger questionnaire. Although we recommend avoiding the term burnout prior to completing the ABQ, discussing the nature of burnout is appropriate following scale completion as part of debriefing procedures.

- *Ensure Confidentiality.* Consistent with usual protocol when administering sport psychology questionnaires, respondents should be informed that coaches, parents, and teammates will not see their completed questionnaire. This not only upholds ethical standards but also assists in ensuring that respondents provide candid answers. Likewise, it is important to communicate that individual responses to the ABQ will not be disclosed in publications; rather, aggregate data based on the entire sample or subsets of a sample will be reported. Having athletes complete the questionnaire in a private setting, providing adequate spacing when administering the scale in a group setting, and separating respondents from coaches and non-participating athletes also assists in protecting confidentiality and minimizes distractions. When possible, having athletes complete the ABQ anonymously or identifying questionnaires only by code will help ensure confidentiality.

- *Minimize Social Desirability.* Socially desirable responses can be minimized by creating an atmosphere in which participants feel comfortable expressing their true feelings and viewpoints. This can be facilitated by emphasizing the importance of answering the questions honestly and by communicating that there are not "right" or "wrong" answers to the questions. To minimize socially desirable responding, we recommend including the following instructions:

  > "Please read each statement carefully and decide if you ever feel this way about your current sport participation. Your current sport participation includes all the training you have completed during this season. Please indicate how often you have had this feeling or thought this season by circling a number 1 to 5, where 1 means "I almost never feel this way" and 5 means "I feel that way most of the time." There are no right or wrong answers, so please answer each question as honestly as you can. Please make sure you answer all items. If you have any questions, feel free to ask."

  When possible, we recommend reading these instructions to respondents when administering the ABQ. This is especially encouraged when the ABQ is administered in a group setting with adolescent samples. When the ABQ is part of a larger survey that makes reading instructions aloud for the ABQ impractical, then the researcher should emphasize the importance of respondents carefully reading the written instructions and asking questions if they have any difficulty understanding them. Finally, the ABQ is designed for research purposes only, and the person administering the questionnaire should not be a coach or person in a position of power over the athlete. The ABQ user's scientific responsibilities, which are presented earlier in this manual, should be reviewed before administering the ABQ.

A final point about administering the ABQ pertains to the appropriateness of having athletes complete the measure via the internet. To our knowledge, one study has explored this issue. Lonsdale, Hodge, and Rose (2006) compared ABQ responses collected by way of the internet and by way of a traditional pencil and paper administration. Adult (i.e., ages 18 to 58 years, mean = 26.5 years) elite athletes from New

Zealand, representing a wide range of sports, were randomly assigned within each gender, by sport group, to either the internet administration or paper and pencil administration via postal mail. Responses to the internet ($n = 117$) and paper and pencil ($n = 97$) solicitations were examined using a series of nested, multigroup confirmatory factor analyses. More specifically, the series of analyses involved progressively constraining features of the factor analytic model (i.e., loadings, then uniquenesses, then variances, then covariances, then intercepts) and assessing degree of change in model fit. No significant change in model fit occured across the steps, providing evidence for the invariance of ABQ factor structure across the internet and paper and pencil groups. Moreover, latent means and reliability coefficients did not differ on any of the ABQ subscales by group, further suggesting that responses to the ABQ completed on the internet are comparable to those provided by traditional means. Lonsdale et al. did note an approximately 10% higher response rate for the online (i.e., 57%) versus postal mail (i.e., 47%) administration. The authors rightly point out that this is but one investigation and that further work will be necessary for confident statements about comparability of these two administration modes. This said, the two administration modes appear comparable and therefore we believe that it is appropriate for researchers to administer the ABQ over the internet. As is the case for paper and pencil administration, care should be taken to minimize response biases when administering the ABQ via the internet. Respondents should be ensured of safe transfer of data over the internet and screens should be used that provide instructions and solicit a response as to whether or not the instructions are understood.

Appropriate ABQ Respondent Samples

The ABQ is designed to assess burnout in competitive athletes. In developing the scale, we sampled female and male athletes from a variety of sports (Raedeke & Smith, 2001). Subsequent research using the ABQ has included both team and individual sport athletes of both genders (e.g., Black & Smith, 2007; Cresswell & Eklund, 2005b; Lonsdale, Hodge, & Jackson, 2007). In addition, the ABQ has been administered to respondents representing a wide age range. Our initial development efforts focused on adolescent and collegiate athletes. Subsequent research evaluating the psychometric properties of the ABQ has predominantly sampled young adults. Thus, the developmental appropriateness of using the ABQ with children and early adolescent youth is unknown. Future research is needed before confident recommendations can be made about the use of the ABQ with these samples.

Chapter 2: The Burnout Construct

Athlete burnout is an important issue based on concerns raised by sport psychologists as well as others in the general sport community, including administrators, coaches, parents, and athletes themselves. Although minimal research has examined the prevalence of burnout (Gustafsson, Kenttä, Hassmén, & Lundqvist, 2007), athletes may be vulnerable to the syndrome due to high training and competitive demands, long training seasons, and sport specialization at young ages. For those experiencing burnout, it comes with a high cost. Burnout is thought to be associated with a variety of negative outcomes, including decreased motivation and sport discontinuation, as well as diminished psychological and physical well-being.

Despite the importance of athlete burnout, the empirical database on this syndrome is underdeveloped. The aim of this chapter is to describe the conceptual framework depicting athlete burnout as a psychological syndrome similar to that described in the work domain. Aligned with this aim, we first discuss the origins of the burnout construct in human services/organizational psychology. Following this discussion, we highlight some of the conceptual ambiguity surrounding the burnout construct and the importance of adequately defining burnout. We then describe Maslach and colleagues' depiction of burnout as a syndrome. This sets the foundation for describing the conceptual underpinnings of the ABQ, as well as a discussion of conceptual issues surrounding the nature of burnout that are still debated today. Finally, this chapter concludes with an overview of the process of developing items for the ABQ.

The Origins of the Burnout Construct

Burnout as a psychosocial construct gained notoriety in the 1970s based on the pioneering descriptions provided by Freudenberger (1974) and Maslach (1976). Freudenberger is generally credited as the first to recognize and name the burnout phenomenon. As a psychiatrist working in alternative institutions such as free clinics, he noted that staff members were vulnerable to experiencing a gradual loss of motivation and commitment that was accompanied by a state of exhaustion. About the same time, Maslach, a social psychologist, began describing burnout in human service workers. Following these early descriptions, several hundred articles on burnout were written between 1974 and 1982 (Miller & Kobelski, 1982). However, in their review of the burnout literature, Perlman and Hartman (1982) counted only five data-based studies that were not narrative case studies. Since the 1980s, the literature base on burnout has continued to grow rapidly. Between 1983 and 1990, almost 1,500 references to burnout appeared in professional magazines, scholarly journals, book chapters, books, and dissertations (Kleiber & Enzmann, 1990, cited in Maslach & Schaufeli, 1993). Today, strong interest in burnout remains (Halbesleben & Buckley, 2004). An early 2008 search of the PsycINFO database using the keyword "burnout" and specifying the year 1991 and later yielded more than 3,500 results.

Early accounts described burnout as a cognitive-emotional reaction to stress, resulting from the chronic demands made on a person's resources (Maslach & Goldberg, 1998). At the same time, researchers and clinicians recognized that burnout involved more than a simple reaction to stress (e.g., see chapters by Burisch, Hallsten, and Pines in Schaufeli, Maslach, & Marek, 1993). Burnout was also linked to a process of becoming disillusioned with involvement and loss of passion. Individuals with high initial motivation, expectations, and commitment who later come to believe that they cannot make a difference were described as the most prone to burnout. For example, Freudenberger and Richelson (1980) depicted burnout as a "state of fatigue or frustration brought about by devotion to a cause, way of life, or relationship that failed to produce the expected reward" (p. 13). Thus, burnout occurs when highly motivated individuals with high expectations and goals invest a considerable amount of themselves in an activity and fail to achieve a sense of success or experience unmet expectations.

Although a majority of the early descriptions of burnout occurred in the human service professions, it was apparent from those descriptions that athletes may be prone to burnout. Sport participation can potentially be stressful due to the demands associated with training and competing. Furthermore, the quest for excellence requires a high level of motivation, and athletes devote a great deal of time and energy to sport participation. As such, athletes have qualities that might make them vulnerable to burnout.

In the years following the early descriptions of burnout in human services, the term burnout began to appear with increasing regularity in the sport setting. Sport psychologists described burnout, provided conceptual discussions of potential antecedents and consequences of burnout, and proposed interventions to prevent its occurrence and alleviate its impact (Dale & Weinberg, 1990; Feigley, 1984; Fender, 1989; Gould, 1993; Henschen, 1990; Rotella, Hanson, & Coop, 1991; Smith, 1986; Yukelson, 1990). Despite these accounts, minimal empirical research on athlete burnout existed, and there was little agreement on how to best define burnout.

Conceptual Ambiguity Surrounding Burnout

In the mid-1990s, when the ABQ was first being developed, a variety of burnout descriptions and definitions had been proffered in empirical papers, position papers, and book chapters in the sport literature (Coakley, 1992; Dale & Weinberg, 1990; Gould, 1993; Schmidt & Stein, 1991; Smith, 1986; Weinberg, 1990). Based on these accounts, a clear understanding of what was meant by the term burnout was difficult to pinpoint. Rather, burnout was a buzzword in the sport community that was used loosely and frequently. Undoubtedly, the term itself is appealing because it captures the experience and feeling of those suffering from it and enables others to conjure a vivid image of what is meant by the term. For example, burnout is like a candle that once glowed brightly, began to flicker, and eventually extinguished or burned out. To many, this metaphor suggests the image of a bright, promising athlete who gets fed up with sport participation and stops competing at what should be the peak of her or his career. Even though the term is intuitively appealing, a precise operational definition that delineates what athlete burnout is, and what it is not, was not always apparent in early descriptions of this phenomenon.

The lack of a clear definition of athlete burnout likely hindered research efforts and the development of a burnout measure that was specific to athletes. The first studies on athlete burnout were quite variable in terms of how burnout was conceptualized. For example, Silva (1990) conceptualized burnout in the context of overtraining and queried athletes on factors related to training stress. Along with questions on overtraining and staleness, he had athletes describe and list the causes and symptoms of burnout. However, it is not evident that burnout was defined for the respondents, making it difficult to understand the context in which the athletes were using the term. As another example, Cohn (1990) asked golfers to recall a time they stopped playing because they were "burned out." The golfers indicated that burnout lasted only 5 to 14 days, a time frame much shorter than expected for a phenomenon considered to be chronic in nature (Shirom, 2005). Athletes were not likely discussing burnout as academicians conceive the construct. Thus, there was little consistency in how the term burnout was used in early studies on this issue.

Using the term athlete burnout without clearly articulating what is meant by the term is problematic in advancing the knowledge base on this issue. The definitional issues faced in sport psychology are similar to those raised by human service/organizational psychology researchers, who recognized that the term burnout holds various meanings, and thus the term itself has the potential to become broad, vague, and overinclusive (Beemsterboer & Baum, 1984; Farber, 1983; Freudenberger, 1983; Kahill, 1988; Maslach, 1982; Starrin, Larsson, & Styrborn, 1990). They warned that this could compromise the credibility of scholarly work on burnout. For example, Morrow (1981), in an article titled "The Burnout of Almost Everyone," noted that "one of the biggest difficulties with the concept of burnout is that it has become faddish and indiscriminate, an item of psychobabble" (p. 84). Similarly, Maslach and Jackson (1984) stated that "because it has a catchy ring to it, burnout is sometimes immediately dismissed as a fad or as pseudoscientific jargon that is all surface flash and no substance" (p. 139). Researchers highlighted that, for burnout to endure as a scholarly concept, it needs to be clearly operationally defined so individuals are discussing the same issue when addressing burnout. (e.g., Beemsterboer & Baum, 1984; Cherniss, 1980; Maslach, 1982).

When the ABQ was first developed, the sport literature on athlete burnout was in the same stage as human service research, when initial accounts of burnout were popularized. Concerns that were voiced in human services/organizational psychology about defining burnout were echoed by sport psychology researchers (Dale & Weinberg, 1990; Fender, 1989). Thus, the essential first step in developing the ABQ was to establish a conceptual foundation for the scale. In that effort, Raedeke (1995, 1997) evaluated whether athlete burnout could be aligned with the work on burnout in human services/organizational psychology. That is, he evaluated whether burnout in human services settings and athlete burnout had a common phenomenological underpinning, rather than presuming that a conceptualization idiosyncratic to sport was necessary. At the same time, he recognized the importance of evaluating whether existing definitions captured the underlying dimensions of burnout when applied to the sport domain. Conceptualizing athlete burnout as a phenomenon similar to a syndrome moved this process forward.

Burnout as a Syndrome

Broadly defined, a syndrome is a constellation of signs and symptoms that occur together and define a condition (Shirom, 2005). In early research efforts, the general aim is to identify characteristic signs and symptoms without necessarily focusing on understanding the precise nature and causes of the condition. As the knowledge base increases, refinements to the description of the syndrome occur, as new evidence emerges delineating what is core and peripheral to its underlying nature (Eklund & Cresswell, 2007; Raedeke, Lunney, & Venables, 2002). Inherent within the description of burnout as a syndrome is that the experiential syndrome should be relevant/constant across a variety of contexts. The specific antecedents of the syndrome may vary across setting, and the exact nature of the contributing factors may vary depending on the unique demands associated with a specific social-environmental context. However, the key features of the syndrome itself should be constant across diverse contexts (Eklund & Cresswell, 2007; Schaufeli & Enzmann, 1998).

In the human services, Maslach and Jackson's (1984) description of burnout as a psychological syndrome characterized by "emotional exhaustion, depersonalization, and reduced personal accomplishment that can occur among individuals who work with people in some capacity" (p. 134) helped clarify the burnout construct and served as a catalyst for research. A key feature of their work on burnout was the delineation of a syndrome with three key dimensions. One dimension, emotional exhaustion, is characterized by feelings of extreme fatigue and emotional overextension resulting from the chronic demands placed on a person. The other two dimensions (i.e., depersonalization and reduced personal accomplishment) reflect negative attitudes toward core aspects of a person's job. Depersonalization represents negative reactions and feelings toward clients, as well as the development of a detached attitude. Whereas depersonalization refers to negative attitudes toward clients, reduced personal accomplishment represents a negative attitude toward oneself in relationship to job performance, particularly regarding one's ability to work successfully with clients. Reduced sense of accomplishment is characterized by perceived ineffectiveness and lack of success in working with people (Maslach et al., 1996).

The Foundation of the ABQ: Defining Athlete Burnout

Although Maslach and Jackson's (1984) definition of burnout is well accepted, they initially limited it to people-oriented occupations where the provider-recipient relationship is central to the job. These professions are characterized by a provider-recipient relationship that occurs in emotionally demanding contexts. Although the emotional exhaustion component readily transfers beyond the human service professions because of its relationship to stress, the other two dimensions, particularly depersonalization, may be less applicable to other domains (Garden, 1987, 1989; Leiter, 1992; Maslach & Schaufeli, 1993). Maslach (1993) warned about overextending the definition of burnout outside of the human services domain and stated that it may be necessary to modify the definition to fit an alternative domain. In applying the multidimensional definition to other domains, Maslach and Schaufeli (1993) stated that researchers should critically assess the core elements of a particular domain (i.e., the central purposes or responsibilities involved in that domain) and customize the burnout dimensions to align with those core elements.

In preliminary efforts to develop the ABQ, Raedeke (1995, 1997) highlighted the need to modify Maslach and Jackson's (1984) burnout definition to adjust for contextual differences between the role of an athlete and that of a human services provider. Although the coach-athlete relationship is characterized by a provider-recipient relationship, athletes are on the receiving end of that relationship. Consequently, the provider-recipient relationship does not define the most central aspect of sport for athletes. The core element of sport for athletes is achieving success at performing athletic skills and obtaining desired outcomes (e.g., learning, improving, mastering sport skills). As such, burnout for athletes should be defined in relation to *sport performance.*

Of the burnout dimensions described by Maslach and Jackson (1984), emotional exhaustion seems the most applicable to athletes. Athletes experiencing burnout may be emotionally exhausted from dealing with continual stresses of competition, training, and other demands for their time (e.g., work, school). Extending the burnout conceptualization beyond emotional exhaustion, athletes may also feel physically exhausted from the chronic physical demands of training, a hallmark of many sports. As with the exhaustion component of burnout, reduced personal accomplishment also appears to be applicable to athletes when defined in terms of sport participation. Athlete burnout may be associated with a sense of reduced personal accomplishment in terms of sport performance and ability. For example, athletes may feel they are training hard yet making minimal progress toward their goals.

The remaining burnout dimension, depersonalization, on the surface appears to be the least applicable to athletes. However, this apparent incompatibility disappears when contextual differences between sport and the human services are considered. Depersonalization represents devaluation of and detachment from what is important in a particular domain. In human service professions, clients are of central importance and depersonalization is represented by a negative and detached attitude toward them. Applied to athletes, Raedeke (1995, 1997) reasoned that depersonalization consists of negative attitudes toward sport and involvement in it.

This dimension is represented by sport devaluation and psychological detachment from sport. Athletes experiencing burnout may stop caring about sport and their performance to the point of developing a resentful attitude toward sport. Thus, in applying Maslach and Jackson's (1984) definition to the sport domain, Raedeke defined athlete burnout as a syndrome of physical/emotional exhaustion, reduced athletic accomplishment, and sport devaluation. These three dimensions are the foundation for the ABQ.

Support for this modified account of burnout is consistent with the extant research examining burnout in work settings outside the human service domain. Maslach and colleagues developed a General Survey version of the Maslach Burnout Inventory (MBI) (Leiter & Schaufeli, 1996; Maslach et al., 1996; Schutte, Toppinen, Kalimo, & Schaufeli, 2000) by modifying the burnout dimensions to more accurately describe the experiential syndrome in general work settings. Emotional exhaustion was extended to include physical exhaustion. The perceived accomplishment scale was recast to assess how effective individuals felt at work, rather than with clients. Depersonalization was reconceptualized as a broader construct of cynicism, depicted by a negative and detached attitude toward one's job. The General Survey version of the MBI did not exist when Raedeke (1995) initiated development of the ABQ, yet both scales converge by including emotional/physical exhaustion, reduced sense of accomplishment or inefficacy, and devaluation or cynicism.

Additional support for the conceptualization of the ABQ stems from qualitative studies on athlete burnout from a variety of sport types. Although not focused on defining burnout, Gould, Tuffey, Udry, and Loehr's (1994, 1996) interviews of tennis players identified as experiencing burnout lend support to the mulitidimensional framework of the ABQ. Tennis players described feeling fatigued, tired, and having low energy, as well as being mentally and emotionally drained. Moreover, they also discussed the central role that unmet expectations and lack of improvement, success, and talent had in their tennis experiences. Aligned with the concept of sport devaluation, the players also reported that tennis became less important to them and that they had a bad attitude toward tennis.

More recently, several studies have been conducted to more directly examine if the multidimensional conceptualization of athlete burnout underlying the ABQ is relevant across a variety of sport types and contexts (Creswell & Eklund, 2006c, 2007; Goodger, Wolfenden, & Lavallee, 2007). For example, Goodger and colleagues interviewed junior tennis players in the United Kingdom to understand athletes' perceptions of key symptoms and consequences associated with each dimension. Their findings supported the multidimensional conceptualization and highlighted overlap and interrelationships among dimensions reflective of a syndrome. Cresswell and Eklund (2006c, 2007) interviewed rugby players in New Zealand and the United Kingdom to evaluate the extent to which the multidimenisonal conceptualization of burnout reflected the experience of athletes from different organizational cultures. They concluded that the experiential characteristics associated with burnout are robust across settings, despite varying situational and environmental demands associated with burnout. Thus, across these qualitative studies, researchers conclude that emotional/physical exhaustion, reduced sense of accomplishment, and devaluation characterize athletes' burnout experiences. However, it should be noted that the researchers conducting these studies were familiar with the multidimensional conceptualization of burnout and selected study participants in part based on elevated ABQ scores. This could have shaped results to favor the specific multidimensional conceptualization on which the ABQ is founded.

Raedeke and colleagues (2002) further supported the conceptual foundation of the ABQ through interviews of USA Swimming coaches. Given that athlete burnout is an important applied issue, in part based on concerns expressed by coaches, the study was designed to examine coaches' perspectives on this issue and how those views compare to academic definitions. Coaches' viewpoints on the nature of burnout, as well as their ideas on causes and prevention of burnout, were examined. A content analysis of their beliefs resulted in swimming burnout being characterized as a withdrawal from swimming, noted by a reduced sense of accomplishment, devaluation/resentment of sport, and physical/psychological exhaustion. Their views on burnout were largely consistent with the multidimensional conceptualization underlying the ABQ. However, much like the qualitative studies on burnout conducted with athletes, the researchers were aware of existing burnout conceptualizations, which may have influenced interpretations of interview results.

Debated Issues in Conceptualizing Burnout

Early reviewers noted that the term "burnout" had become a catchword used to represent almost any sign of distress, discontent, and negative response to stress (Carroll & White, 1982; Cordes & Dougherty, 1993; Kahill, 1988). For example, Burisch (1993) noted more than 130 symptoms associated with the term "burnout." Inherent in the description of burnout as a syndrome is debate as to what is central and less central to this phenomenon. Based on the principle of parsimony, striving for the smallest number of central characteristics that adequately describe burnout and have theoretical meaning is important. Although defining athlete burnout in terms of exhaustion, reduced sense of accomplishment, and devaluation is consistent with the most widely accepted conceptualization within organizational psychology, it is important to acknowledge that considerable debate on the exact nature of this syndrome still exists today (Cox, Tisserand, & Taris, 2005).

Since the earliest accounts of burnout, there has been nearly unanimous agreement that burnout is a cognitive-emotional reaction to stress, characterized by high levels of exhaustion resulting from the chronic demands made on a person's resources (e.g., Cherniss, 1980; Cordes & Dougherty, 1993; MacNeil, 1981; Maslach, 1993; Perlman & Hartman, 1982; Shirom, 1989). Given the central role of exhaustion, there has been some debate centering on whether burnout should be defined as a unidimensional concept based on exhaustion or in multidimensional terms (Cox, Kuk, & Leiter, 1993; Evans & Fischer, 1993; Shirom, 1989). Pines and Aronson (1988) defined burnout as "a state of physical, emotional, and mental exhaustion caused by long-term involvement in situations that are emotionally demanding" (p. 9) and developed a unidimensional measure subsuming the physical, emotional, and mental elements under the umbrella construct of exhaustion. Others advocating that exhaustion is central to the burnout process have suggested that depersonalization and reduced personal accomplishment are related to burnout but are not core aspects of the experience itself (Koeske & Koeske, 1989, 1993). More recently, Kristensen, Borritz, Villadsen, and Christensen (2005) developed the Copenhagen Burnout Inventory, which focuses on feelings of fatigue and exhaustion. In doing so, they argue that a reduced sense of accomplishment is a consequence of exhaustion and that depersonalization is a coping strategy but not part of the burnout syndrome itself.

On the other side of this debate, scholars have argued that defining burnout exclusively in terms of exhaustion deprives burnout of its contextual richness (Maslach et al., 2001; Schaufeli & Taris, 2005). Numerous constructs in psychology (e.g., depression, hopelessness, chronic fatigue, stress) and sport (e.g., overtraining syndrome) are characterized by fatigue and exhaustion. Defining burnout exclusively in terms of exhaustion makes it difficult to differentiate burnout from such constructs, whereas coupling exhaustion with depersonalization/cynicism and reduced personal accomplishment is more unique to burnout. Thus, a multidimensional view provides a richer description of burnout and differentiates burnout from stress and other related constructs (Jackson, Schwab, & Schuler, 1986; Leiter, 1991, 1993; Maslach, 1993).

Despite the debate surrounding burnout as a unidimenisonal or multidimensional construct, most concur that emotional exhaustion represents the core and the most validated dimension of burnout (Cox et al., 1993; Gaines & Jermier, 1983; Shirom, 1989; Wallace & Brinkerhoff, 1991). Stronger correlations of self-diagnoses of burnout with emotional exhaustion have been observed than with depersonalization or reduced personal accomplishment. Moreover, individuals use signs of exhaustion, but not reduced personal accomplishment and depersonalization, to define burnout in other individuals (Pick & Leiter, 1991; Rafferty, Lemkau, Purdy, & Rudisill, 1986). Consistent with this finding, an item including the word "burnout" is included on the exhaustion subscale of the MBI. Furthermore, an item containing the word "burnout" that was included in a questionnaire administered to a subsample of athletes from Raedeke's (1995) dissertation research loaded most strongly on the exhaustion factor of a preliminary version of the ABQ in an exploratory factor analysis. Thus, emotional exhaustion appears to be the salient aspect of burnout when individuals rate burnout in themselves or others.

Aside from this debate on the centrality of exhaustion to burnout, the nature of exhaustion itself is debated. Given that both emotional and physical exhaustion are highlighted in our definition of athlete burnout, emotional and physical exhaustion could be construed as distinct components of the burnout syndrome (see Lonsdale, Hodge, & Jackson, 2007, for a discussion of this issue). It is possible that physical exhaustion is linked to sport training demands, whereas emotional exhaustion is associated with psychosocial stressors. We combined these aspects of exhaustion when developing the ABQ to create a parsimonious representation of burnout. Although emotional and physical exhaustion might be conceptually differentiated, we believe they are likely integrated and indistinguishable in experiential terms by athletes suffering from burnout. This is in accord with other burnout measures, where emotional, physical, and mental fatigue are subsumed under the unidimensional umbrella term of exhaustion (e.g., Halbesleben & Demerouti, 2005; Pines & Aronson, 1988).

Following exhaustion, devaluation/cynicism is the most widely accepted dimension. The role of perceived accomplishment is less clear (Cox, Tisserand, & Taris, 2005). Reflecting back on early fatigue research, Schaufeli and Taris (2005) argued that burnout can be described in terms of the ability and willingness to expend effort.

Specifically, exhaustion depicts the ability to expand effort and devaluation/cynicism represents the willingness to expend effort. Reduced accomplishment is not considered central to the experiential syndrome but instead an antecedent or a consequence of burnout. Others have also questioned the role of a reduced sense of accomplishment (e.g., Kalliath, O'Driscoll, Gillespie, & Bluedorn, 2000; Schaufeli & Taris, 2005). Aligned with these views, the Oldenburg Burnout Inventory focuses on exhaustion and disengagement (Halbesleben & Demerouti, 2005). Exhaustion is thought to develop from high job demands, whereas disengagement is conceptually similar to devaluation/cynicism and thought to stem from a lack of job-related resources.

In contrast to these views, qualitative work by sport psychology researchers has highlighted that reduced sense of accomplishment is a core dimension of burnout in the sport setting (e.g., Goodger, Wolfenden, & Lavallee, 2007; Gustafsson, Kenttä, Hassmén, Lundqvist, & Durand-Bush, 2007; Gustafsson, Hassmén, Kenttä, & Johansson, in press). This possibly reflects contextual differences between sport and some work domains. For athletes, performance is the central concern, as their accomplishments are continually being evaluated by themselves and others. Therefore, it appears important to address reduced sense of accomplishment when seeking to measure the burnout syndrome in athletes.

Another issue that is not well understood by burnout researchers is whether the burnout dimensions develop in a sequential order. For example, Leiter and Maslach (1988) suggest that, in response to high levels of stress and emotional exhaustion, a person copes by developing a detached attitude toward clients. As a consequence of depersonalization, the human service provider is not as effective in working with clients, contributing to development of a reduced sense of personal accomplishment. Lee and Ashforth (1993) suggest that heightened exhaustion leads to both depersonalization and a reduced sense of accomplishment. More recently, Maslach and colleagues argue that emotional exhaustion develops first in response to stress and that depersonalization/cynicism develops subsequently as a result. A reduced sense of accomplishment is thought to develop independently and in parallel to the other dimensions (Maslach & Goldberg, 1998; Maslach et al., 2001).

Not all researchers agree that emotional exhaustion is the first burnout dimension to develop. For example, Golembiewski, Munzenrider, and Carter (1983) suggest that depersonalization is the first aspect of burnout to develop. Alternatively, Taris, Le Blanc, Schaufeli, and Schreurs (2005) contend that none of the models positing sequential relationships between burnout components are well supported. Rather, they suggest that a reciprocal relationship exists between some of the burnout dimensions. For example, based on longitudinal data, they found that higher exhaustion leads to depersonalization and reduced accomplishment, yet depersonalization also leads to higher exhaustion. It is also important to note that the strength of these time-lagged effects was small. Thus, while recognizing the central role of exhaustion, it is entirely possible that an invariant sequencing of the emergence of burnout dimensions does not exist and that the burnout dimensions are reciprocally related to one another. Indeed, qualitative work on athlete burnout suggests that the syndrome shows considerable diversity in its evolution (Gould, Tuffey et al., 2006; Gustafsson, Kenttä, Hassmén, Lundqvist, & Durand-Bush, 2007; Gustafsson et al., in press).

Debate and diversity in scholarly viewpoints on what is central to burnout is certainly healthy and aligned with viewing burnout as a syndrome. Given that the term athlete burnout is associated with a wide variety of meanings, the first step in developing a measure was to operationally define the construct. In doing so, Raedeke recognized that athlete burnout shared similarities with the syndrome as described in work settings but may have unique features as well. Our goal was to develop a measure that captured the essence of this syndrome for athletes. We also recognized the importance of not creating an idiosyncratic definition of athlete burnout that unintentionally contributed to conceptual ambiguity surrounding the general burnout construct. Thus, we modeled our definition of athlete burnout after a widely supported conceptualization in work settings, forwarding it as an experiential syndrome of emotional/physical exhaustion, reduced sense of accomplishment, and sport devaluation.

Preliminary Item Development

The ABQ is based on a multidimensional conceptualization of athlete burnout that includes emotional/physical exhaustion, reduced sense of accomplishment, and sport devaluation dimensions. In deriving items to tap these dimensions, Raedeke (1995, 1997) examined existing measures, including the Maslach Burnout Inventory (Maslach & Jackson, 1981) for human services, the unidimensional Burnout Measure (Pines & Aronson, 1988) based on exhaustion, and the Eades Athlete Burnout Inventory (Eades, 1990). Results from Gould, Tuffey et al.'s (1994) qualitative study of tennis burnout were also examined as a potential basis of content for ABQ items. Raedeke (1995, 1997) then created a large pool of potential items by writing new items based on the operational definition of each burnout dimension and modifying/adapting items from existing sources.

Emotional and physical exhaustion items were developed to assess emotional fatigue stemming from the psychological demands associated with sport as well as physical exhaustion from the intense physical demands associated with training and competing. Sources of fatigue, such as excessive training/inadequate recovery, were not included in item content to ensure that items assessed the experiential state of exhaustion, not contributing factors. Similarly, reduced sense of accomplishment items were developed in relationship to sport performance and ability, not factors contributing to this experiential state such as performance plateaus, lack of improvement, or failure to achieve goals. Finally, sport devaluation items were developed to capture a negative, detached attitude toward sport, reflected by lack of concern about sport and performance quality. Items reflecting potential affective changes associated with sport devaluation, such as feelings of depression, were not included.

After developing a large item pool, seven items for each athlete burnout dimension were selected that most closely reflected the respective operational definitions and that covered the breadth of each dimension with minimal overlap/redundancy across items. An additional consideration in item selection was the extent to which items might evoke socially desirable responses or result in response set biases, such as participants not using the complete item response range. A sport psychologist with expertise in motivation was consulted for feedback during the process of selecting items. Three sport psychology graduate students then rated each item for logical validity and readability. After modifying items based on their feedback, a sample ($n = 7$) of high school swimmers pilot tested the questionnaire for item readability and comprehension. Their suggestions were used in modifying item wording.

The ABQ item response format is similar to that of both Eades' (1990) and Maslach et al.'s (1996) inventories in that burnout is assessed in terms of frequency of occurrence. Although Maslach and Jackson (1981) originally included both frequency and intensity ratings, Maslach (Maslach, 1993; Maslach et al., 1996) later recommended including only the frequency response set because of redundancy between the two sets of ratings. The specific foils of the ABQ differ from those used in Eades' and Maslach and Jackson's inventories. For example, the MBI foils are: (0) *never*, (1) *a few times a year or less*, (2) *once a month or less*, (3) *a few times a month*, (4) *once a week*, (5) *a few times a week*, and (6) *everyday*. In contrast, the ABQ foils are: (1) *almost never*, (2) *rarely*, (3) *sometimes*, (4) *frequently*, and (5) *most of the time*. This modification was implemented to make it easier for athletes to respond to the questionnaire and because not all athletes train throughout the entire year.

In summary, we have overviewed conceptual perspectives, ambiguity, and debates that ultimately must be considered in making judgments about the burnout construct and the validity evidence surrounding the ABQ. We have also described our process for developing ABQ items. This definitional stage of construct validation serves as the base on which confirmatory and theory-testing stages of the validation process are built (Rowe & Mahar, 2006). Efforts reflecting these validation stages are presented in the following two chapters, which cover within-network and between-network validation efforts, respectively.

Chapter 3: Within-Network Validation

The ultimate goal in the scale development process is to develop a set of items whose measurement properties support construct validity (AERA, 1999; Clark & Watson, 1995; Marsh, 1998; Messick, 1995; Rowe & Mahar, 2006; Zumbo, 2005). Construct validity is the extent to which scores derived from a measurement tool assess the construct it is designed to assess rather than some other construct. Evaluating construct validity is an ongoing process that involves examining several different sources of evidence. This chapter addresses within-network validation evidence, describing the dimensionality of the ABQ by summarizing results from studies that employ exploratory and confirmatory factor analysis as well as studies that report intercorrelations of burnout dimensions. Results of multitrait-multimethod work on the ABQ are also discussed. Finally, given the central role of reliability in evaluating measurement quality, a description of both internal consistency and stability of ABQ scores is included in this chapter.

Evaluation of a Preliminary Version of the ABQ

The first study to examine the factor structure and internal consistency of ABQ items (Raedeke & Smith, 2001, Study 1) used data collected as part of Raedeke's (1995) dissertation research that was subsequently published in a study examining a sport commitment perspective on burnout (Raedeke, 1997). Participants were 236 senior age-group swimmers (145 female, 84 male, 7 unspecified), ages 13 to 18 years ($M = 15.5$, $SD = 1.5$). The swimmers were recruited in the state of Oregon and most were White (94%). The sample was highly involved in swimming. Participants had swam competitively an average of 6.4 years (range = 1–14, $SD = 2.8$) and trained 10.6 months of the year ($SD = 1.8$), on average. Each week they spent nearly 14 hours ($M = 13.7$, $SD = 4.9$) in training activities, across slightly more than seven sessions ($M = 7.2$, $SD = 2.3$), and swam nearly 40,000 yards ($M = 39,795$, $SD = 17,775$).

To examine whether the 21 ABQ items conformed to the multidimensional operational definition of burnout, a principal axis factor analysis was conducted. Both varimax and oblimin rotations yielded similar solutions. Given low to moderate correlations among factors (range = .11 to .46) and easier interpretability, results from the varimax rotation were interpreted. Four factors had eigenvalues greater than 1.0 in the initial extraction with the four-factor solution accounting for 59% of the common item variance. Item loadings of .40 or greater were considered meaningful in interpreting factors. Table 3.1 includes the factor loadings, alpha coefficients, eigenvalues, and variance percentages.

The first two factors corresponded to the sport devaluation and emotional/physical exhaustion dimensions, respectively. Items focusing on reduced sense of swimming accomplishment split into two factors. Rather than reflecting two distinguishable concepts, the reduced sense of accomplishment items appeared to divide into two factors because of item wording. With one exception, the positively worded personal accomplishment items (reversed scored) loaded on one factor and the negatively worded items loaded on the other factor. Four items were complex, loading on more than one factor, and one item failed to load on any factor (see Table 3.1).

Evaluation of the Factor Structure of a Revised ABQ

In revising the ABQ (Raedeke & Smith, 2001, Study 2), we sought to develop a measure containing a core of five items for each component of burnout to keep the ABQ relatively short in length, yet long enough to adequately reflect each burnout dimension. To accomplish this, we examined results from our evaluation of the preliminary version, attained consensus between us on the acceptability of items, and solicited feedback from a panel of graduate students with expertise in sport psychology and/or swimming. The graduate student panelists were provided with the burnout dimension descriptions and were asked to evaluate how well each item from the preliminary ABQ reflected its respective dimension. The panelists were also asked to indicate which five of the seven items best represented the breadth of the content for each dimension and to comment on readability of items. Based on panel feedback, very minor wording modifications were made to some items. Finally, we rewrote two items and developed three new items. These five "trial" items were included at the end of the measure and were to be used as replacement items if any core items showed poor psychometric qualities.

To evaluate the factor structure of the revised ABQ, a sample of swimmers was recruited from swimming clubs in five different U.S. states to complete the ABQ (Raedeke & Smith, 2001, Study 2). Respondents were 244 senior age-group swimmers (131 female, 112 male, 1 unspecified), ages 14 to 19 years ($M = 15.8$, $SD = 1.3$), most of whom were White (94%). They had competed in swimming for 8.0 ($SD =$

Table 3.1: Factor Loadings of Burnout Items for the Preliminary Version of the ABQ

Item	| Factor Loadings			
	1	2	3	4
Swimming Devaluation (α = .89)				
Swimming is less important to me than it used to be	**.87**	.18	.27	.05
I don't care as much about my swim performance as I used to	**.79**	.13	.20	.17
I'm just not into swimming like I used to be	**.76**	.17	.25	.16
I feel less concerned about being successful in swimming than I used to	**.76**	.13	.07	.26
The effort I spend in swimming would be better spent doing other things	**.61**	.37	.12	-.05
Sometimes I wonder if swimming is worth all the time and energy I put into it	**.47**	**.43**	.23	.06
I feel swimming is positively influencing my life	.39	.13	.07	.12
Emotional/Physical Exhaustion (α = .89)				
I feel physically worn out from swimming	.12	**.78**	.15	.12
I feel overly tired from swim team participation	.19	**.78**	.01	.04
I just feel like I don't have any energy	.13	**.74**	.21	.09
I feel so tired from my training that I have trouble finding energy to do other things	.06	**.71**	-.05	-.02
I feel "wiped out" from swimming	.36	**.62**	.29	.06
I feel fatigued when I think about having to go to practice	.39	**.56**	.23	.04
I feel emotionally drained from my swim participation	**.41**	**.54**	.29	.12
Reduced Sense of Swimming Accomplishment (α = .84)				
It seems no matter what I do, I don't swim as well as I should	.14	.21	**.77**	.13
I am not performing up to my ability in swimming	.25	.06	**.68**	.21
I feel successful at swimming	.27	.14	**.57**	**.52**
I don't feel confident about my swim ability	.19	.16	**.56**	.29
My swimming is really going downhill	**.43**	.16	**.44**	.14
Sense of Swimming Accomplishment (α = .78)				
I have accomplished many worthwhile things in swimming	.25	.04	.24	**.79**
I've done well at meeting the goals I've set for myself in swimming	.12	.10	.39	**.63**
Eigenvalue (final solution)	8.1	2.2	1.5	0.6
Percent of variance (final solution)	38.5	10.5	6.9	2.9

Note: Factor loadings > .40 appear in bold font.

Reprinted, with permission, from Raedeke, T. D., & Smith, A. L. (2001). Development and preliminary validation of an athlete burnout measure. *Journal of Sport & Exercise Psychology, 23*(4), 286.

2.9) years on average, trained 10.5 ($SD = 1.1$) months per year, and completed 19.0 ($SD = 6.1$) hours per week in training activities. The median weekly swimming volume reported by study participants was 50,000 meters ($SD = 22,200$).

Confirmatory factor analysis (CFA) using LISREL 8 (Scientific Software International) was conducted, specifying the hypothesized multidimensional factor structure of burnout underlying the ABQ. Initially, descriptive statistics including skewness and kurtosis values were examined for ABQ items (see Table 3.2). All item scores were reasonably normally distributed, evident by univariate skewness ($M = 0.44$, $SD = 0.30$) and kurtosis ($M = -0.34$, $SD = 0.21$) values that did not exceed an absolute value of 1. The combined core and trial burnout items, however, demonstrated significant multivariate skewness (Mardia's coefficient = 43.4) and kurtosis (Mardia's coefficient = 14.1). Despite the availability of estimation techniques for non-normal data, we opted to employ maximum likelihood estimation because this statistical estimation procedure has been demonstrated to generally perform well with non-normal data (see Chou & Bentler, 1995; Hu & Bentler, 1998).

Aligned with conventional guidelines for interpreting CFA results, we examined a variety of absolute and incremental indices to judge overall model fit. We used χ^2, where a nonsignificant value means that the observed data are consistent with the proposed model. However, it is not unusual for χ^2 to be significant and lead to rejection of adequately fitting models. Therefore, we placed greater weight on the goodness of fit index (GFI), nonnormed fit index (NNFI), comparative fit index (CFI), and root mean square error of approximation (RMSEA) in judging model fit. In general, scores of .90 or higher on the fit indexes and .08 or lower on the RMSEA represent acceptable fit based on traditional guidelines (Byrne, 1998). More recently, Hu and Bentler (1999) have recommended a .95 cutoff for NNFI and CFI and a .06 cutoff for the RMSEA, though Marsh, Hau, and Wen (2004) caution researchers against applying these criteria as "golden rules."

A first-order, three-factor model consistent with the multidimensional conceptualization of burnout was tested, with scores on the core items serving as the observed indicators. This model exhibited an acceptable fit to the data (see Table 3.3). Examination of the modification indices indicated that two items (i.e., 12 from emotional/physical exhaustion and 15 from devaluation) were complex. Therefore, three additional models were run. We initially evaluated whether replacing item 12 (i.e., "I feel like I don't have any energy for swimming") with trial item 16 (i.e., "I feel emotionally drained from swimming") improved model fit. No improvement in model fit was observed, and modification indices also showed item 16 to be complex. Consequently, in the second revised model, we replaced item 12 with item 17

Table 3.2: Descriptive Statistics for Core and Trial Items of the Revised ABQ (Raedeke & Smith, 2001, Study 2)

		Descriptive Statistics		
Item	Mean	SD	Skew	Kurt
Emotional/Physical Exhaustion				
2. I feel so tired from my training that I have trouble finding energy to do other things	3.27	0.98	-.11	-.45
4. I feel overly tired from my swim participation	3.00	1.02	.11	-.35
8. I feel "wiped out" from swimming	3.16	0.97	.03	-.38
10. I feel physically worn out from swimming	3.16	1.03	-.03	-.25
12. I feel like I don't have any energy for swimming	2.49	0.99	.29	-.28
16. *I feel emotionally drained from swimming*	2.30	1.12	.63	-.26
17. *I am exhausted by the mental and physical demands of swimming*	2.71	1.01	.31	-.30
Reduced Sense of Accomplishment				
1. I'm accomplishing many worthwhile things in swimming	2.05	0.81	.43	-.11
5. I don't feel confident about my swim ability	2.21	1.04	.54	-.33
7. I am not performing up to my ability in swimming	2.52	1.11	.44	-.47
13. It seems that no matter what I do, I don't swim as well as I should	2.53	1.20	.41	-.80
14. I feel successful at swimming	2.17	0.90	.30	-.58
18. *I am not achieving much in swimming*	2.00	0.98	.84	.10
20. *I feel I've done well in swimming*	1.93	0.87	.66	.15
Sport Devaluation				
3. The effort I spend in swimming would be better spent doing other things	2.15	0.94	.48	-.37
6. I don't care as much about my swim performance as I used to	2.14	1.26	.95	-.16
9. I'm not into swimming like I used to be	2.27	1.28	.73	-.57
11. I feel less concerned about being successful in swimming than I used to	2.14	1.17	.82	-.23
15. I wonder if swimming is worth all the time and energy I put into it	2.64	1.09	.16	-.64
19. *I have negative feelings toward swimming*	2.28	1.13	.72	-.14

Notes: Trial items italicized. Items 1, 14, and 20 are reverse scored.

(i.e., "I am exhausted by the mental and physical demands of swimming"), the other emotional/physical exhaustion trial item. Fit indices improved, and there was no cross-loading problem. We therefore retained item 17 and omitted item 12. In the third revised model, we replaced item 15 (i.e., "I wonder if swimming is worth all the time and energy I put into it") with item 19 (i.e., "I have negative feelings toward swimming"), the alternative devaluation trial item. Fit indices were improved, and there was no cross-loading problem. All key parameter estimates (i.e., factor loadings, interfactor correlations, and uniquenesses) were significant at the $p < .05$ level. This model was retained as the final ABQ model for this study.

Table 3.3: *Confirmatory Factor Analysis Fit Indices for the Revised ABQ Model (Raedeke & Smith, 2001, Study 2)*

Model	χ^2	df	p	GFI	NNFI	CFI	RMSEA
First-order, three-factor	244.2	87	<.01	.88	.90	.92	.086
Replaced item 12 with item 17	198.7	87	<.01	.90	.93	.94	.073
Replaced item 15 with item 19	188.9	87	<.01	.90	.94	.95	.069

Interfactor correlations within the final model were moderately large ($\phi = .52$ to .71). Given these correlations, other factor combinations may have represented the data as well as the model we specified. Therefore, we tested four plausible alternative models. First, we examined a first-order, univariate model, which exhibited a poor fit to the data that significantly departed from the model we specified, $\Delta\chi^2(3) = 494.3$, $p < .05$. The remaining models were first-order, two-factor models in which two burnout dimensions were represented by one latent variable. The fits of these models were also significantly worse than our base three-factor model, range $\Delta\chi^2(2) = 159.0$ to 370.2, all $p < .05$. Overall, results from this study showed the a priori factor structure that we specified fit the ABQ scores well, particularly after replacing two core items with trial items.

The next study (Raedeke & Smith, 2001, Study 3) was designed to cross-validate the ABQ model stemming from the previous study with a sample of athletes representing a variety of sport types. Because initial scale development efforts occurred within the swimming context, it was unknown whether the ABQ would be applicable to other sport settings. For this evaluation of the ABQ, 208 collegiate athletes (133 female, 75 male), ages 17 to 23 years ($M = 19.6$, $SD = 1.3$), were recruited from Division I and II institutions in the Midwest and Southeast. Athletes were sampled from a variety of team and individual sports including basketball ($n = 11$), cross-country running ($n = 49$), soccer ($n = 86$), softball ($n = 21$), tennis ($n = 13$), track and field ($n = 16$), and volleyball ($n = 12$). White (89%) and Black (7%) respondents comprised most of the sample, with the remaining respondents distributed across a variety of racial backgrounds. On average the athletes practiced/trained 14.2 ($SD = 6.0$) hours per week over 10.5 ($SD = 2.2$) months of the year.

Participants completed the final 15-item version of the ABQ from the previous study. In addition, one trial item for each burnout component was included at the end of the questionnaire in the event that any core items showed poor psychometric qualities. Examination of univariate descriptive statistics for each item revealed that skewness ($M = 0.46$, $SD = 0.32$) and kurtosis ($M = -0.21$, $SD = 0.29$) values did not exceed an absolute value of 1. The combined core and trial burnout items demonstrated significant multivariate skewness (Mardia's coefficient = 35.7) and kurtosis (Mardia's coefficient = 10.7); however, we opted to use maximum likelihood estimation, as in the previous study, when conducting CFAs. Descriptive statistics for the core and trial burnout items appear in Table 3.4.

The final first-order, three-factor model from the previous study exhibited a good fit to the scores from the sample of college athletes (see Table 3.5). Though modification indices did not point to any theoretically sound modifications, item 5 (i.e., "I don't feel confident about my [*sport*] ability") from the reduced sense of accomplishment subscale exhibited a low squared multiple correlation value ($R^2 = .13$) relative to the other items ($R^2 = .47$ to .77). We therefore reran the model with the reduced sense of accomplishment trial item 17 (i.e., "I am not achieving much in [*sport*]") replacing item 5. This model also fit the data well, all parameter estimates were significant at the $p < .05$ level (see Table 3.6 for standardized factor loadings and uniquenesses), and the squared multiple correlation value of the trial item ($R^2 = .66$) was better aligned with the other items. Therefore, we retained the trial item and omitted item 5 in finalizing the ABQ model. Because interfactor correlations were moderately large ($\phi = .32$ to .67), we tested alternative models as in the previous study. The first-order, one-factor model ($\Delta\chi^2(3) = 645.0$, $p < .05$) and first-order, two-factor models (range $\Delta\chi^2(2) = 178.7$ to 430.2, all $p < .05$) exhibited significantly worse fit than our final ABQ model.

Overall, findings from this study supported the item replacements from the previous study. Given the additional item replacement in this study, we conducted a post hoc examination of the replacement with data from the previous swimming sample (the trial item was used in both studies). The trial item exhibited a stronger loading

Table 3.4: Descriptive Statistics for Core and Trial Items of the ABQ Administered to College Athletes (Raedeke & Smith, 2001, Study 3)

Item	Mean	SD	Skew	Kurt
<u>Emotional/Physical Exhaustion</u>				
2. I feel so tired from my training that I have trouble finding energy to do other things	2.93	0.93	-.11	-.22
4. I feel overly tired from my [sport] participation	2.52	0.99	.28	-.32
8. I feel "wiped out" from [sport]	2.51	1.03	.16	-.60
10. I feel physically worn out from [sport]	2.57	1.01	.13	-.54
12. I am exhausted by the mental and physical demands of [sport]	2.56	1.03	.25	-.36
16. *I feel mentally and physically drained from* [sport]	2.51	1.01	.22	-.32
<u>Reduced Sense of Accomplishment</u>				
1. I'm accomplishing many worthwhile things in [sport]	2.00	0.86	.46	-.53
5. I don't feel confident about my [sport] ability	2.48	1.05	.55	.03
7. I am not performing up to my ability in [sport]	2.86	1.04	.15	-.40
13. It seems that no matter what I do, I don't perform as well as I should	2.53	1.00	.26	-.27
14. I feel successful at [sport]	2.38	0.92	.39	-.14
17. *I am not achieving much in* [sport]	2.05	0.95	.58	-.30
<u>Sport Devaluation</u>				
3. The effort I spend in [sport] would be better spent doing other things	1.92	0.93	.85	.39
6. I don't care as much about my [sport] performance as I used to	2.03	1.16	.95	.04
9. I'm not into [sport] like I used to be	2.08	1.14	.75	-.50
11. I feel less concerned about being successful in [sport] than I used to	2.03	1.03	.89	.25
15. I have negative feelings toward [sport]	2.04	0.91	.57	-.12
18. *[Sport] is less important to me than it used to be*	2.02	1.09	.94	.17

Notes. Trial items italicized. [sport] replaced with specific sport of respondent. Items 1 and 14 are reverse scored.

than the original item on the reduced sense of accomplishment factor (standardized $\lambda = .79$ versus .65) and did not cross load on the other factors. This supported the scale modification and retention of the replacement item in the final ABQ model. The ABQ as is currently used appears in Appendix A, followed by scoring instructions in Appendix B.

Table 3.5: *Confirmatory Factor Analysis Fit Indices for the Final ABQ Model (Raedeke & Smith, 2001, Study 3)*

Model	χ2	df	p	GFI	NNFI	CFI	RMSEA
First-order, three-factor	155.3	87	<.01	.91	.95	.96	.062
Replaced item 5 with item 17	149.7	87	<.01	.91	.96	.97	.060

Table 3.6: *Standardized Factor Loadings and Uniquenesses for the Final ABQ Model (Raedeke & Smith, 2001, Studies 2 and 3)*

Item	Study 2 λ	Study 2 θ	Study 3 λ	Study 3 θ
Emotional/Physical Exhaustion				
2. I feel so tired from my training that I have trouble finding energy to do other things	.72	.48	.75	.44
4. I feel overly tired from my [sport] participation	.76	.42	.85	.28
8. I feel "wiped out" from [sport]	.82	.33	.83	.31
10. I feel physically worn out from [sport]	.77	.41	.85	.28
12. I am exhausted by the mental and physical demands of [sport]	.77	.41	.85	.28
Reduced Sense of Accomplishment				
1. I'm accomplishing many worthwhile things in [sport]	.70	.51	.71	.49
5. I am not achieving much in [sport]	–	–	.81	.35
7. I am not performing up to my ability in [sport]	.78	.39	.67	.56
13. It seems that no matter what I do, I don't perform as well as I should	.71	.50	.73	.47
14. I feel successful at [sport]	.75	.43	.74	.45
Sport Devaluation				
3. The effort I spend in [sport] would be better spent doing other things	.57	.68	.70	.50
6. I don't care as much about my [sport] performance as I used to	.82	.34	.84	.29
9. I'm not into [sport] like I used to be	.90	.19	.88	.23
11. I feel less concerned about being successful in [sport] than I used to	.83	.31	.83	.31
15. I have negative feelings toward [sport]	.67	.55	.76	.43

Note: Items are from final ABQ model from Raedeke & Smith (2001) Study 3

Subsequent to our publication of the ABQ (Raedeke & Smith, 2001), others have evaluated the factor structure of the ABQ. We highlight the work of Lonsdale and colleagues (Lonsdale, 2005; Lonsdale et al., 2006; Lonsdale, Hodge, & Jackson, 2007) because they evaluated the ABQ without incorporating other constructs into their measurement model, allowing a direct comparison to our original work. In a study comparing online ($n = 117$) and postal mail ($n = 97$) responses to the ABQ from New Zealand athletes (M age = 26.5 years) participating in a variety of sports, Lonsdale and colleagues (2006) found marginal to acceptable fit of the ABQ model for both administration modes (see Table 3.7). Further testing showed the model to be invariant across online and postal administrations. Using data from his dissertation research (Lonsdale, 2005) and published as part of a larger study on athlete engagement (Lonsdale, Hodge, & Jackson, 2007), the ABQ measurement model showed an acceptable fit to scores collected online from 343 New Zealand athletes from a variety of sports (see Table 3.7). Item factor loadings were significant at the $p < .05$ level and ranged from .58 to .89 (standardized). Overall, the research to date on the ABQ supports the proposed factor structure underlying ABQ scores.

Table 3.7: Confirmatory Factor Analysis Fit Indices for the Final ABQ Model (Lonsdale, 2005; Lonsdale et al., 2006)

Model	χ^2	df	TLI/NNFI	CFI	RMSEA
Lonsdale et al. (2006) – Online	172.4	87	.89	.91	.09
Lonsdale et al. (2006) – Postal	213.1	87	.90	.92	.11
Lonsdale (2005)	239.2	87	.92	.93	.07

Reliability and Scale Intercorrelations

Across studies, ABQ scores have demonstrated strong internal consistency reliability. In the initial scale development process, alpha coefficients ranged from .84 to .91 across burnout dimensions (i.e., α = .88/.91 for emotional/physical exhaustion, .84/.85 for reduced sense of accomplishment, and .87/.90 for devaluation in Raedeke & Smith, 2001, Studies 2 & 3). Across subsequent studies, alpha coefficients have ranged from .70 to .91 with values typically exceeding .80 (Black & Smith, 2007; Creswell & Eklund, 2004, 2005a, 2005b; Lemyre, Treasure, & Roberts, 2006; Lonsdale et al., 2006; Lonsdale, Hodge, & Jackson, 2007).

In addition to strong internal consistency reliability, ABQ scores have demonstrated test-retest reliability over seven to nine days in a subsample of 25 cross-country runners

(Raedeke & Smith, 2001, Study 3). Test-retest values for each of the subscales indicate the stability of scores derived from the ABQ: emotional/physical exhaustion ($R = .92$), reduced sense of accomplishment ($R = .86$), and sport devaluation ($R = .92$).

Consistent with conceptualizing burnout as a syndrome, correlations among ABQ dimensions are in the moderate range. Latent interfactor correlations in Raedeke and Smith's (2001) Studies 2 and 3 show values of $\phi = .54$ and .32 between emotional/physical exhaustion and reduced sense of accomplishment, $\phi = .52$ and .53 between emotional/physical exhaustion and devaluation, and $\phi = .71$ and .67 between reduced sense of accomplishment and devaluation.

Subsequent to our initial scale development efforts, several researchers have reported Pearson r correlations or latent variable correlations among ABQ dimensions. In general, moderate correlations among burnout dimensions have been observed (Black & Smith, 2007; Cresswell & Eklund, 2005a, 2005b, 2005c, 2006a; Lemyre et al., 2006; Lonsdale, Hodge, & Jackson, 2007). Most often, the highest interrelationship is between reduced sense of accomplishment and sport devaluation, with a typical correlation of about .60 (range from .47 to .74). Given that both of these variables are attitudinal in nature, and emotional/physical exhaustion is more psychophysiological, this is an unsurprising observation. Exhaustion and devaluation are also moderately associated, with the typical correlation about .53 (range from .35 to .68). Finally, the weakest relationship is found between exhaustion and reduced sense of accomplishment, with a correlation generally about .35 (range from .21 to .56).

Multitrait-Multimethod Evaluation of the ABQ

In addition to examining dimensionality and reliability, another approach to construct validation involves a multitrait-multimethod (MTMM) analysis. This approach allows examination of whether a measure is more strongly related to an alternative measure of the same construct and more weakly related to measures assessing conceptually distinct constructs (Rowe & Mahar, 2006). This enables a simultaneous evaluation of both convergent and discriminant validity. Using this approach, Creswell and Eklund (2006b) examined the construct validity of the ABQ, as well as the Maslach Burnout Inventory–General Survey (MBI-GS; Maslach et al., 1996). Both measures specifically referred to rugby, as participants ($N = 392$) were New Zealand premier male amateur rugby players (ages 18 to 42 years, mean = 25.3 years). Participants completed the burnout measures along with depression and anxiety inventories, which are affective constructs conceptually related to, but not redundant with, burnout. Conceptually, the two burnout measures should be strongly related with each other and differentiated from depression and anxiety. A series of confirmatory factor analyses, structured within an MTMM framework as described in Byrne (1994), were conducted with attention to relative fit across models and parameter estimate values.

Relative to one another, the ABQ and the MBI-GS demonstrated convergent validity and adequate discriminant validity. In support of convergent and internal discriminant validity, conceptually matching subscales (e.g., ABQ emotional/physical exhaustion with MBI-GS exhaustion) showed latent intercorrelations of |.64| to |.73|, whereas conceptually non-matching subscales across the measures showed values of |.24| to |.53|. Both burnout measures also exhibited appropriate discriminant validity relative to depression and anxiety, showing low to moderate latent intercorrelations (range = |.22| to |.60|). The MBI-GS displayed slightly weaker results in comparison to the ABQ, primarily because of difficulties with the MBI-GS cynicism scale that were not observed with the corresponding ABQ devaluation scale. Overall, the researchers concluded that their results supported the continued use of the ABQ in sport settings.

In summary, our own research and that conducted by other researchers supports the construct validity of scores derived from the ABQ using a within-network approach. Both exploratory and confirmatory factor analysis results aligned with the hypothesized multidimensional structure of the ABQ, which includes the dimensions of emotional/physical exhaustion, reduced sense of personal accomplishment, and sport devaluation. In addition, intercorrelations of ABQ dimensions are generally in the moderate range, and subscale scores have demonstrated internal consistency and test-retest reliability. Finally, an MTMM evaluation of the ABQ also supports its construct validity.

Chapter 4: Between-Network Validation

Although the athlete burnout literature is not extensive, there has been intensified activity in the research area over recent years (see Eklund & Cresswell, 2007; Goodger, Gorely, Lavallee, & Harwood, 2007; Smith, Lemyre, & Raedeke, 2007). In Chapter 3, we reviewed research examining the ABQ from a within-network approach to accumulating validity evidence. This chapter reviews validity evidence from a between-network approach. This involves assessing the relationship of ABQ scores with scores reflecting other variables to assess if a theoretically predicted pattern of relationships exists. Several studies have used the ABQ to explore associations of burnout dimensions with theoretically related constructs. We briefly review these efforts below. The overview is delimited to published research using the English version of the ABQ. From these investigations, correlations between ABQ subscale scores and theoretically associated constructs are included in Table 4.1, which offers a comparative overview of evidence for the between-network validity of the dimensions underlying the ABQ.

Burnout in sport, as well as other settings, is widely viewed as a reaction to chronic stress resulting from the demands made on a person's resources (Maslach et al., 2001; Smith, 1986). Thus, burnout is expected to be positively associated with perceived stress and to be related to a variety of personal and situational factors associated with the stress process (see Lazarus, 1990; Smith, 1986). During the development of the ABQ, in addition to assessing its factor structure, Raedeke and Smith (2001, Study 2) examined correlations between ABQ subscales and perceived stress, coping resources, and social support. Perceived stress was expected to positively associate with burnout, whereas coping resources and social support satisfaction were hypothesized to negatively associate with burnout subscales. These hypotheses were supported in a sample of adolescent competitive swimmers. Specifically, Raedeke and Smith found that perceived stress was positively correlated with the ABQ subscales (r = .43 to .63). Furthermore, they found that coping resources (r = -.20 to -.29) and social support (r = -.24 to -.31) exhibited significant negative correlations with the ABQ subscales. Later examination of these data showed that the

Table 4.1: Correlations of ABQ Subscale Scores with Theoretically Related Constructs

Source	Sample
Black & Smith (2007)	182 competitive swimmers; female and male; ages 13 to 22 yrs.; United States
Cresswell & Eklund (2004)[a]	199 professional rugby union players; male; ages 19 to 33 yrs.; New Zealand
Cresswell & Eklund (2005c)	Same
Cresswell & Eklund (2005a)	102 professional rugby union players; male; ages 19 to 32 yrs.; New Zealand
Cresswell & Eklund (2005b)[bc]	392 premier division amateur rugby union players; male; ages 18 to 42 yrs.; New Zealand
Cresswell & Eklund (2006b)[b]	Same
Lemyre et al. (2006)	44 elite swimmers; female and male; ages 18 to 24 yrs.; United States
Lonsdale, Hodge, & Jackson (2007, Study 3)	343 athletes from New Zealand Academy of Sport; range of sports; female and male; Age = 24.5±7.7 yrs.

	ABQ Subscale		
Construct/Variable	Emot/Phys Exhaust	Reduced Accomplish	Sport Devaluation
swim competence	.07	-.23	-.12
weekly yardage	.20	-.22	-.02
perceived stress	.39	.64	.51
swim identity strength	-.03	-.36	-.34
swim identity exclusivity	.11	-.24	-.27
participation control	-.25	-.24	-.40
day-to-day control	-.13	-.17	-.17
money hassles	.04	.21	.04
rugby hassles	.46	.17	.26
social support	-.17	-.42	-.30
intrinsic mot - accomplish	-.03	-.26	-.30
external regulation	-.12	-.08	-.07
amotivation	.19	.40	.60
intrinsic mot - accomplish	-.11	-.30	-.28
identified regulation	-.07	-.18	-.13
introjected regulation	.02	-.02	-.08
external motivation	.09	-.09	-.08
amotivation	.25	.45	.52
intrinsic motivation	-.12	-.19	-.27
external regulation	-.05	.04	-.05
amotivation	.31	.56	.61
anxiety	.39	.40	.34
depression	.57	.45	.57
self-determination trend[d]	-.30	-.39	-.54
negative affect swings	.53	.50	.40
positive affect swings	.39	.04	.10
dedication	-.14	-.53	-.65
confidence	-.19	-.65	-.41
vigor	-.37	-.53	-.49
enthusiasm	-.32	-.53	-.66

Table 4.1: Correlations of ABQ Subscale Scores with Theoretically Related Constructs, continued

Source	Sample
Price & Weiss (2000)[e]	193 high school varsity soccer players; female; ages 14 to 18 yrs.; United States
Raedeke (1997)[e]	236 competitive swimmers; female and male; ages 13 to 18 yrs.; United States
Raedeke & Smith (2001, Study 2)[f]	244 competitive swimmers; female and male; ages 14 to 19 yrs.; United States
Raedeke & Smith (2001, Study 3)	208 intercollegiate athletes; range of sports; female and male; ages 17 to 23 yrs.; United States

Notes: Underlined correlations not significant at $p < .05$ level. CTA = competitive trait anxiety. [a]Rugby competence and control scales not reliable and therefore not included here. [b]Latent variable correlations reported. [c]ABQ item 4 removed from exhaustion subscale. [d]Direction of correlations are in error in original source but corrected here following personal communication with lead author. [e]A preliminary version of the ABQ was used in this study. [f]One ABQ item on reduced sense of accomplishment scale different from final version of ABQ.

	ABQ Subscale		
Construct/Variable	Emot/Phys Exhaust	Reduced Accomplish	Sport Devaluation
perceived competence	-.22	-.51	-.33
anxiety	.39	.67	.36
enjoyment	-.31	-.48	-.64
p. coach training & instruct	-.05	-.20	-.12
p. coach democratic	-.32	-.32	-.24
p. coach autocratic	.19	.20	.22
p. coach social support	-.14	-.11	-.09
p. coach positive feedback	-.13	-.27	-.24
enjoyment	-.49	-.39	-.64
benefits	-.52	-.45	-.65
costs	.57	.40	.52
alternative attractiveness	.53	.35	.67
investments	-.21	-.38	-.50
social constraints	.47	.34	.42
swim identity	-.31	-.30	-.53
perceived control	-.49	-.44	-.54
stress	.48	.63	.43
coping	-.20	-.29	-.23
social support	-.31	-.28	-.24
enjoyment	-.36	-.36	-.61
intrinsic mot – stimulation	-.20	-.24	-.45
intrinsic mot – accomplish	-.20	-.22	-.40
intrinsic mot – know	-.18	-.19	-.35
identified regulation	-.06	-.02	-.17
amotivation	.46	.66	.68
CTA–somatic	.20	.22	.14
CTA–worry	.24	.46	.20
CTA–concentration disrupt	.19	.40	.31
enjoyment	-.40	-.41	-.61
commitment	-.37	-.51	-.76
intrinsic mot – stimulation	-.22	-.31	-.45
intrinsic mot – accomplish	-.23	-.34	-.45
intrinsic mot – know	-.26	-.46	-.51
identified regulation	-.00	-.24	-.10
introjected regulation	.02	.01	.02
external regulation	.03	-.15	-.02
amotivation	.31	.57	.64

associations of coping resources and social support with burnout were mediated by stress, supporting the view that coping resources and social support influence burnout by way of their influence on stress perceptions (Raedeke & Smith, 2004). Other researchers have also found ABQ subscales to negatively correlate with social support (Cresswell & Eklund, 2004) and to positively associate with stressors such as injury and non-selection, as well as perceived sport-related hassles in rugby union players (Cresswell & Eklund, 2004, 2006a). In combination, these investigations show ABQ scores are consistent with predictions stemming from a stress-based burnout framework.

In addition to lifestyle factors and stressors, individual characteristics such as trait anxiety play an important role in stress-related processes and, thus, are theoretically related to burnout. In a study of college athletes from a variety of sports, Raedeke and Smith (2001, Study 3) found that ABQ subscales positively and significantly related to somatic ($r = .14$ to $.22$), worry ($r = .20$ to $.46$), and concentration disruption ($r = .19$ to $.40$) components of competitive trait anxiety, with the strongest relationships existing between the reduced accomplishment ABQ scores and the worry and concentration disruption trait anxiety scores. Other work corroborates this link between anxiety and burnout, particularly with regard to reduced sense of accomplishment perceptions (Price & Weiss, 2000; Wiggins, Cremades, Lai, Lee, & Erdmann, 2006). For example, Wiggins and colleagues showed that athletes perceiving anxiety as facilitative exhibited lower reduced accomplishment scores than those perceiving anxiety as debilitative.

Negative affective states are conceptually linked to stress and therefore are expected to positively relate with burnout perceptions. In a longitudinal examination of elite swimmers spanning a swim season, swings in negative affect predicted burnout perceptions at season's end for all ABQ subscales (Lemyre et al., 2006). Combined with Cresswell and Eklund's (2006b) work showing burnout to be associated with depression and anxiety in high-level amateur rugby union players, these investigations suggest a robust link between ABQ subscale scores and negative affective states. Overall, research efforts have shown ABQ scores are associated with stress-related constructs in theoretically expected directions and, thus, support the construct validity of the ABQ.

Although a stress-based perspective has been the most common framework for studying burnout, sport researchers have considered alternative frameworks for understanding this phenomenon. Coakley (1992) forwarded a sociological perspective connecting burnout in adolescent athletes to the social organization of intensive sport participation. Due to the social structure of sport, athletes may experience limited control over their endeavors and may develop a narrowed or unidimensional identity. Specifically, Coakley suggested that the social organization of sport prevents adolescent athletes from having meaningful control over their sport involvement at an age when it becomes increasingly important for them to develop a sense of autonomy. Moreover, athletes may not explore roles outside of being an athlete because of the time demands associated with intensive sport participation. As a result, athletes may define themselves exclusively as athletes, rather than adopting the multifaceted identity more typical of adolescents.

In an empirical examination of Coakley's perspective, Black and Smith (2007) measured swimming competence, stress-based variables (i.e., weekly training yardage, perceived swimming stress), perceived control, athletic identity strength and exclusivity, and burnout in adolescent competitive swimmers. In support of the perspective, they found that perceived control and athletic identity exclusivity explained variance in ABQ subscale scores over and above that explained by swimming competence and stress-based variables. Perceived stress was positively related to ABQ subscales ($r = .39$ to $.64$). Lower perceived control over one's swimming participation associated with higher burnout responses as expected ($r = -.24$ to $-.40$). Also, lower perceived control of day-to-day aspects of swimming involvement associated with higher reduced accomplishment and devaluation scores (both $r = -.17$), although the correlations were weak. These findings are consistent with those of Cresswell and Eklund (2004), who found a variety of perceived control items to correlate negatively with ABQ subscales in professional rugby union players. They were also consistent with those of Raedeke (1997), who examined adolescent competitive swimmers and found a global perceived control measure to correlate negatively with subscale scores from a preliminary version of the ABQ. Finally, the findings are in line with work by Price and Weiss (2000), who found that female adolescent soccer players holding higher perceptions of coach democratic behavior (i.e., supporting athlete control) scored lower on burnout perceptions. An opposite pattern of findings emerged relative to players' perceptions of autocratic (i.e., controlling) behavior on the part of their coaches.

Contrary to expectations, Black and Smith (2007) found higher athletic identity exclusivity to associate with lower reduced accomplishment ($r = -.24$) and devaluation ($r = -.27$) scores. The unexpected direction of identity exclusivity findings was attributed by the authors to the nature of the identity measure and the cross-sectional design of the study, which did not capture how athletes arrived at their respective identity exclusivity levels. An exclusive identity is not expected to be maladaptive if it follows the exploration of various life directions; however, it can be maladaptive when other life directions are not explored and circumstances within that domain change (Marcia, 1994; Marcia, Waterman, Matteson, Archer, & Orlofsky, 1993). When an athlete is satisfied with how sport is going, a unidimensional athletic identity will not be problematic, and exclusivity is reflective of identity strength, how closely one identifies with the role of being an athlete. Identity strength and exclusivity correlated at .70 in Black and Smith's study. When an athlete perceives that sport is not going as well as it once was, the relation of these identity constructs with burnout may diverge. Identity strength would decline because the athlete experiencing burnout begins the process of devaluing sport. However, exclusivity would not necessarily decline because alternative identities have not been developed. Thus, higher exclusivity would associate with higher burnout scores at this stage of the burnout process, whereas identity strength and burnout scores would continue to inversely track. A key issue here is that the nature of the relationship between identity exclusivity and burnout may depend on the stage of the burnout process experienced by the athlete. Overall, the existing perceived control findings provide support for the validity of the ABQ, whereas identity findings are difficult to interpret without a longitudinal process-oriented design that captures how athletes develop their identity and the potentially dynamic relationship between identity and burnout.

In addition to Coakley's (1992) sociological perspective, sport psychologists have complemented stress-based perspectives on burnout by emphasizing the link of motivational constructs with burnout (e.g., Cresswell & Eklund, 2005b; Gould, 1996; Gould, Udry, Tuffey, & Loehr, 1996; Raedeke, 1997). In fact, the first study (i.e., Raedeke, 1995, 1997) to test the relationship between burnout and theoretically related constructs using the ABQ was based on a motivational framework emphasizing commitment (Schmidt & Stein, 1991). Based on this perspective, athletes can be committed to sport for a combination of reasons related to "wanting to be involved" and "feeling they have to be involved." Entrapment occurs when athletes do not want to participate in sport but feel they have to maintain their sport involvement. Theoretically, this occurs when athletes experience low enjoyment coupled with low benefits and high costs. Despite this unfavorable view of sport, athletes may maintain involvement because of high investments (too much invested to quit), high social constraints (others expect them to maintain their involvement), and lack of attractive alternatives to sport participation. Integrating Coakley's perspective with a commitment perspective, Raedeke suggested that low control and a unidimensional identity may also serve as sources of entrapment when an athlete's attraction to sport is declining. Characteristics associated with entrapment are theoretically associated with burnout. Using cluster analysis, Raedeke found four profiles of athletes that he labeled enthusiastic, malcontented, obligated, and indifferent. Swimmers belonging to the groups labeled malcontented and obligated had some characteristics associated with entrapment, and their burnout scores were higher than those swimmers in the enthusiastic and indifferent groups. Though some of the findings (i.e., investments, identity, and attractiveness of alternatives) within the multivariate profiles were only partially aligned with theoretical expectations, these results are difficult to interpret within the cross-sectional design that was employed. Relationships of these variables and burnout may vary by the stage of the burnout process that is experienced by an athlete. This is also reflected in the univariate level correlations, which showed burnout scores to be negatively associated with enjoyment, benefits, personal investments, swim identity, and perceived control and positively associated with costs, attractiveness of alternatives to swimming, and social constraints.

Burnout is often characterized as a shift from passionate engagement in sport to involvement that is underpinned by an absence of or low motivation, if not withdrawal from sport altogether (Cresswell & Eklund, 2005b; Gould, 1996). In their examination of competitive adolescent swimmers, Raedeke and Smith (2001, Study 2) explored the link of ABQ subscales with enjoyment, a marker of adaptive motivation, and various forms of motivation that vary in the degree to which they are self determined. Self-determination pertains to human functioning that is driven by one's own choices (Deci & Ryan, 1985). The forms of motivation that were measured fall on a continuum from intrinsic motivation, reflective of participating in an activity for the innate pleasure and satisfaction of involvement, to extrinsic types of motivation, reflecting the pursuit of behavior as a means to some end, and amotivation (i.e., without motivation), where respondents cannot ascribe reasons for involvement in an activity (see Deci & Ryan, 1985; Pelletier et al., 1995). Burnout would be expected to negatively correlate with intrinsic motivation and to positively correlate with amotivation. The extrinsic forms of motivation falling on the continuum between these endpoints would be expected to show weaker correlations with burnout. Consistent with expectations, ABQ subscale scores correlated negatively with enjoyment ($r = -.36$ to $-.61$) and intrinsic motivation ($r = -.18$ to $-.45$) indices, whereas ABQ scores correlated positively with amotivation scores ($r = .46$ to $.68$). The strongest relationships were with the devaluation subscale, which is expected given the nature of this burnout dimension. Also consistent with expectations, scores on the extrinsic form of motivation reliably assessed in this study, identified regulation, did not correlate with the emotional/physical exhaustion or reduced accomplishment scores and showed a weak correlation with devaluation ($r = -.17$).

In Raedeke and Smith's (2001, Study 3) examination of college athletes, these relational patterns were corroborated. Enjoyment ($r = -.40$ to $-.61$), intrinsic motivation indices ($r = -.22$ to $-.51$), and amotivation ($r = .31$ to $.64$) exhibited significant associations with ABQ subscales. Scores on subscales tapping three forms of extrinsic motivation showed no significant association with emotional/physical exhaustion or devaluation ABQ scores. Significant correlations of small magnitude were found for identified regulation ($r = -.24$) and external regulation ($r = -.15$) aspects of extrinsic motivation with reduced accomplishment ABQ scores. This study also included an assessment of enjoyment-based sport commitment, which, as expected, demonstrated negative correlations with ABQ subscales ($r = -.37$ to $-.76$).

This pattern of relationships between ABQ subscales and various types of motivation has been observed in several other studies, with the trend revealing that amotivation is the most strongly associated with burnout, with correlations typically of medium to large magnitude. Various types of extrinsic motivation are unrelated or weakly related to burnout scores. Intrinsic motivation indices show significant correlations of small magnitude with scores on the devaluation and reduced sense of accomplishment subscales but less consistently show a significant association with exhaustion scores (Cresswell & Eklund, 2005a, 2005b, 2005c). Furthermore, Lemyre and colleagues (2006) showed that elite swimmers with a declining trend of self-determined motivation across a season report higher end-of-season ABQ scores than those with an increasing trend of self-determined motivation. Collectively, these investigations suggest that ABQ scores correspond with conceptual views on the link between burnout and motivation.

Recent work by Lonsdale and his colleagues has focused on the definition and measurement of athlete engagement, a construct considered to be the antithesis of burnout. Based on qualitative data from a range of high performance athletes, Lonsdale, Hodge, and Raedeke (2007) defined athlete engagement as a persistent, positive, cognitive-affective experience in sport that is characterized by confidence, dedication, and vigor. Lonsdale, Hodge, and Jackson (2007) followed this effort by designing a measure of athlete engagement that resulted in a survey instrument containing confidence, dedication, and vigor subscales, as well as an enthusiasm subscale. As part of this research, they examined the relationship between athlete engagement and burnout among high performance athletes from New Zealand participating in a variety of sport types (see Study 3). Generally, the latent relationships between conceptually bipolar burnout and engagement dimensions were strong (i.e., devaluation and dedication/enthusiasm $\phi = -.79$ and $-.80$, respectively, reduced accomplishment and confidence $\phi = -.79$, exhaustion and vigor $\phi = -.42$). Scores on engagement and burnout dimensions of greatest conceptual correspondence showed higher intercorrelations than noncorresponding dimensions. For example, confidence showed a higher correlation with reduced accomplishment than did dedication, vigor, and enthusiasm. This work further strengthens the case for ABQ scores possessing good between-network validity.

Overall, ABQ subscales exhibit theoretically expected relationships with measures of various constructs drawn from stress, sociological, and motivational perspectives on athlete burnout. We believe this reflects well on the efficacy of the ABQ as a tool to assess athlete burnout. However, validation of scores derived from a psychometric instrument is an ongoing process, and a relatively small number of studies using the ABQ have been published to date. ABQ users will need to carefully review future published research investigations on athlete burnout to form judgments about the conceptual and psychometric strengths and weaknesses of this measure.

Chapter 5: ABQ Score Profiles

Among the most frequently asked questions about athlete burnout and the ABQ are: (a) how prevalent is the burnout syndrome? and (b) how does one interpret the magnitude of ABQ scores? Discussion surrounding the prevalence of burnout has appeared in the sport psychology literature (e.g., Gustafsson, Kenttä, Hassmén, & Lundqvist, 2007; Eklund & Cresswell, 2007), with consensus that much more research is necessary to shed light on this issue. Two challenges in addressing this question by using ABQ scores are that burnout is multidimensional and it is conceptualized as being continuous, rather than dichotomous, in nature. There is no diagnostic threshold for ABQ scores that is indicative of the state conceptualization of burnout (i.e., burned out versus not burned out). This is consistent with work psychology research, where only preliminary efforts have been undertaken to assess the clinical significance of burnout scores (e.g., Schaufeli, Bakker, Hoogduin, Schaap, & Kladler, 2001). Thus, interpretation of ABQ scores will largely rest on evaluation of the magnitude of scores, for which there are no formal norms. The aim of this chapter is to provide readers with basic descriptive information on scores derived from the ABQ in existing research. We believe this will assist researchers in interpreting ABQ scores, though we remind readers that validation of ABQ scores is an ongoing process that is in a relatively early stage. Within this chapter, we report means and standard deviations of ABQ subscale scores that are reported in published research investigations using the English version of the ABQ. We then pool data from several of these investigations and report descriptive information for the total collection of participants as well as subgroups by gender, age, and type of sport.

Table 5.1 contains means and standard deviations by subscale for studies that have used the ABQ. Examination of these data reveals a few trends. First, scores on ABQ subscales are consistently patterned across investigations. Athletes most frequently perceive emotional/physical exhaustion, followed by reduced sense of accomplishment, and then sport devaluation. Second, in one of the two studies reporting ABQ scores across time (Cresswell & Eklund, 2005a), there appear to be slight increases in burnout perceptions over the course of a rugby tournament. These increases do not appear to exist in research by the same authors that explored ABQ scores over a full rugby year (Cresswell & Eklund, 2006a). Clearly, further investigation is neces-

Table 5.1: Means and Standard Deviations by Subscale for Published Studies using the ABQ

Source	Sample
Black & Smith (2007)	182 competitive swimmers; female and male; ages 13 to 22 yrs.; United States
Cresswell & Eklund (2004, 2005c)	199 professional rugby union players; male; ages 19 to 33 yrs.; New Zealand

Cresswell & Eklund (2005a)	102 professional rugby union players; male; ages 19 to 32 yrs.; New Zealand
	    Pre-tournament
	    Mid-tournament
	    Post-tournament

Cresswell & Eklund (2005b, 2006b)	392 premier division amateur rugby union players; male; ages 18 to 42 yrs.; New Zealand

Cresswell & Eklund (2006a)	109 professional rugby union players; male; ages 19 to 32 yrs.; New Zealand
	    Pre-competitive year
	    During competitive year
	    End of competitive year

Lemyre et al. (2006)	44 elite swimmers; female and male; ages 18 to 24 yrs.; United States

Lonsdale, Hodge, & Rose (2006)	214 athletes from New Zealand Academy of Sport; range of sports; female and male; ages 18 to 58 yrs.
	    Online respondents ($n = 117$)
	    Postal respondents ($n = 97$)

Lonsdale, Hodge, & Jackson (2007, Study 3)	343 athletes from New Zealand Academy of Sport; range of sports; female and male; age = 24.5±7.7 yrs.
Price & Weiss (2000)[a]	193 varsity high school soccer players; female; ages 14 to 18 years; United States
Raedeke (1997)[a]	236 competitive swimmers; female and male; ages 13 to 18 yrs.; United States

	ABQ Subscale	
Emot/Phys Exhaust M(SD)	Reduced Accomplish M(SD)	Sport Devaluation M(SD)
2.92(0.89)	2.29(0.81)	1.99(0.90)
2.32(0.72)	2.43(0.68)	2.16(0.76)
2.39(0.57)	2.04(0.44)	1.65(0.53)
2.36(0.63)	2.23(0.52)	1.82(0.67)
2.43(0.58)	2.50(1.17)	1.90(0.67)
2.32(0.72)	2.43(0.67)	2.16(0.77)
2.57(0.48)	2.09(0.53)	1.82(0.59)
2.34(0.60)	2.27(0.61)	1.81(0.62)
2.49(0.54)	2.29(0.53)	1.87(0.65)
2.88(0.92)	2.50(0.92)	1.92(0.82)
3.00(0.69)	2.29(0.73)	2.21(0.65)
3.20(0.67)	2.23(0.74)	2.05(0.69)
2.70(0.76)	2.26(0.71)	1.97(0.76)
2.59(0.92)	2.56(0.87)	2.11(0.90)
2.47(0.83)	2.32(0.74)	2.02(0.84)

Table 5.1: Means and Standard Deviations by Subscale for Published Studies using the ABQ, continued

Source	Sample
Raedeke & Smith (2001, Study 2; 2004)[b]	244 competitive swimmers; female and male; ages 14 to 19 yrs.; United States
Raedeke & Smith (2001, Study 3)	208 intercollegiate athletes; range of sports; female and male; ages 17 to 23 yrs.; United States

Notes: [a]A preliminary version of the ABQ was used in this study. [b]One ABQ item on reduced sense of accomplishment scale different from final version of ABQ.

sary that tracks ABQ scores over time to gain a better understanding of the burnout process (Goodger, Wolfenden, & Lavallee, 2007; Gustafsson, Kenttä, Hassmén, Lundqvist, & Durand-Bush, 2007). Third, relative to the response set options, the average scores overwhelmingly fall in the *rarely* to *sometimes* range, suggesting that most athletes are not experiencing burnout perceptions on a regular basis. Finally, the standard deviations are reasonably consistent across studies and are of sufficient magnitude to suggest that some athletes *almost never* experience feelings or thoughts reflecting burnout, whereas others experience such feelings or thoughts to a degree that is likely maladaptive.

In addition to presenting previously published descriptive information on ABQ subscale scores, we contacted all authors who have published data using the English version of the ABQ and requested their data so that we may provide further information to readers on typical ABQ responses. We were able to secure seven data sets, for a total of 1,627 athlete respondents (Black & Smith, 2007; Cresswell & Eklund, 2005b, 2006b; Lonsdale et al., 2006; Lonsdale, Hodge, & Jackson, 2007; Lemyre et al., 2006; Raedeke & Smith, 2001, 2004). This total sample contains 680 female and 946 male respondents (one athlete did not specify gender). There are 426 athletes from studies that predominantly employed adolescent respondents, whereas the remaining 1,201 athletes are from studies that predominantly examined college age and/or older respondents. The sample consists of 847 individual sport and 747 team sport athletes (sport type was unknown for 33 athletes). Of the individual sport athletes, 517 are swimmers. Similarly, the team sport sample is heavily represented by rugby

ABQ Subscale		
Emot/Phys Exhaust M(SD)	Reduced Accomplish M(SD)	Sport Devaluation M(SD)
3.06(0.82)	2.30(0.79)	2.19(0.95)
2.62(0.86)	2.37(0.76)	2.02(0.88)

players ($n = 423$). We also categorized the athletes as involved in sports that are physical conditioning intensive ($n = 1,341$; e.g., swimming, rugby) or not conditioning intensive ($n = 253$; e.g., bowls, shooting).

Two general approaches have been used to interpret burnout inventory scores. One approach used by Maslach et al. (1996) with the MBI has been to develop norms by dividing the distribution into thirds with scores in the upper third defined as high burnout, those in the middle third as average burnout, and those in the bottom third reflecting low burnout. Table 5.2 contains means and standard deviations, as well as the one-third and two-thirds cutoff points for ABQ scores on each subscale. This information is provided for the total sample, as well as the subgroups described above. Across groups there is consistency for reduced sense of accomplishment and devaluation scores, whereas it appears that adolescent, individual sport, and female athletes may experience slightly more frequent emotional/physical exhaustion than college/adult, team sport, and male athletes, respectively. Based on the two-thirds cutoff values, a general rule of thumb when using this approach to interpreting burnout scores would be that a score of about 3, corresponding to "sometimes" on the ABQ response set, or higher signifies relatively high burnout.

The other approach to interpreting burnout scores is to consider scores relative to the response set options, which represent how frequently an athlete experiences thoughts and feelings indicative of burnout. Table 5.3 contains the percentage of athlete scores falling within a specified range on each ABQ subscale, with that range

Table 5.2: Means, Standard Deviations, and Tertial Cutoff Values for ABQ Subscale by Group

Group ABQ Dimension	M(SD)	1/3 Cutoff	2/3 Cutoff
Total Sample (N = 1,627)			
Emotional/Physical Exhaustion	2.69(0.84)	2.40	3.00
Reduced Sense of Accomplishment	2.32(0.75)	2.00	2.60
Sport Devaluation	2.06(0.83)	1.60	2.40
Female (n = 680)			
Emotional/Physical Exhaustion	2.81(0.85)	2.40	3.20
Reduced Sense of Accomplishment	2.39(0.77)	2.00	2.80
Sport Devaluation	2.09(0.87)	1.60	2.40
Male (n = 946)			
Emotional/Physical Exhaustion	2.60(0.82)	2.20	3.00
Reduced Sense of Accomplishment	2.27(0.72)	2.00	2.60
Sport Devaluation	2.03(0.79)	1.60	2.40
Adolescent (n = 426)			
Emotional/Physical Exhaustion	3.00(0.85)	2.60	3.20
Reduced Sense of Accomplishment	2.27(0.81)	1.80	2.60
Sport Devaluation	2.11(0.93)	1.40	2.40
College/Adult (n = 1,201)			
Emotional/Physical Exhaustion	2.58(0.80)	2.20	3.00
Reduced Sense of Accomplishment	2.34(0.72)	2.00	2.60
Sport Devaluation	2.04(0.79)	1.60	2.40
Individual Sport (n = 847)			
Emotional/Physical Exhaustion	2.83(0.87)	2.40	3.20
Reduced Sense of Accomplishment	2.31(0.79)	1.80	2.60
Sport Devaluation	2.04(0.87)	1.40	2.40
Team Sport (n = 747)			
Emotional/Physical Exhaustion	2.53(0.77)	2.20	2.80
Reduced Sense of Accomplishment	2.37(0.68)	2.00	2.60
Sport Devaluation	2.09(0.78)	1.60	2.40
Conditioning Intensive (n = 1,341)			
Emotional/Physical Exhaustion	2.71(0.85)	2.40	3.00
Reduced Sense of Accomplishment	2.33(0.76)	2.00	2.60
Sport Devaluation	2.07(0.84)	1.60	2.40

Table 5.2: Means, Standard Deviations, and Tertial Cutoff Values for ABQ Subscale by Group, continued

Group ABQ Dimension	M(SD)	1/3 Cutoff	2/3 Cutoff
Not Conditioning Intensive (n = 253)			
Emotional/Physical Exhaustion	2.58(0.73)	2.20	3.00
Reduced Sense of Accomplishment	2.39(0.65)	2.00	2.67
Sport Devaluation	2.04(0.79)	1.60	2.40

Note: Gender information missing for one case, and sport information missing for 33 cases.

corresponding to response set anchors of (1) *almost never*, (2) *rarely*, (3) *sometimes*, (4) *frequently*, and (5) *almost always*. Overall, the greatest proportion of emotional/physical exhaustion and reduced sense of accomplishment scores falls within the range of two to less than three, whereas the greatest proportion of devaluation scores is below two. This holds across all groups except for female respondents and adolescent respondents who, consistent with the means reported in Table 5.2, have the greatest proportion of emotional/physical exhaustion scores falling within the range of three to less than four. A relatively small proportion of respondents report a score of 4 to 5 on any of the ABQ subscales.

Some researchers report the proportion of athletes scoring above a certain level of the response set across all three ABQ subscales (see Eklund & Cresswell, 2007; Price & Weiss, 2000), as this may reflect the strongest experience of the burnout syndrome. Table 5.4 contains the number of respondents with means scores on all ABQ subscales of 3 or greater, as well as 4 or greater. Overall, a small proportion of athletes are in these respective categories, with 6.9% of respondents scoring 3 or greater on all subscales and 0.3% scoring 4 or greater.

These approaches to facilitating score interpretation offer useful information; however, they also clearly have limitations. Given that no diagnostic criteria or theoretical framework exists for interpreting the magnitude of ABQ scores, existing cutoff strategies are somewhat arbitrary. Based on a normative distribution, by definition, 33% of the population falls into each of the low, average, and high categories. Likewise, developing cutoffs based on the actual response set anchors is somewhat arbitrary, as resultant scores are likely affected by a variety of response set influences (e.g., social desirability, sport culture influences, personality differences) and thus cannot be interpreted literally. The cutoff corresponding to what is labeled

Table 5.3: Respondents Scoring within Specified ABQ Subscale Range by Group

Group Subscale Score	Emotional/ Physical Exhaustion freq.	%	Reduced Sense of Accomplishment freq.	%	Sport Devaluation freq.	%
Total Sample ($N = 1,627$)						
1 to <2	272	16.7	503	30.9	792	48.7
2 to <3	702	43.1	759	46.7	576	35.4
3 to <4	519	31.9	330	20.3	208	12.8
4 to 5	134	8.2	35	2.2	51	3.1
Female ($n = 680$)						
1 to <2	98	14.4	198	29.1	323	47.5
2 to <3	255	37.5	312	45.9	240	35.3
3 to <4	256	37.6	147	21.6	85	12.5
4 to 5	71	10.4	23	3.4	32	4.7
Male ($n = 946$)						
1 to <2	174	18.4	304	32.1	469	49.6
2 to <3	447	47.3	447	47.3	335	35.4
3 to <4	262	27.7	183	19.3	123	13.0
4 to 5	63	6.7	12	1.3	19	2.0
Adolescent ($n = 426$)						
1 to <2	39	9.2	159	37.3	208	48.8
2 to <3	158	37.1	167	39.2	139	32.6
3 to <4	166	39.0	88	20.7	52	12.2
4 to 5	63	14.8	12	2.8	27	6.3
College/Adult ($n = 1,201$)						
1 to <2	233	19.4	344	28.6	584	48.6
2 to <3	544	45.3	592	49.3	437	36.4
3 to <4	353	29.4	242	20.1	156	13.0
4 to 5	71	5.9	23	1.9	24	2.0
Individual Sport ($n = 847$)						
1 to <2	111	13.1	289	34.1	439	51.8
2 to <3	338	39.9	365	43.1	273	32.2
3 to <4	298	35.2	165	19.5	99	11.7
4 to 5	100	11.8	28	3.3	36	4.3

Table 5.3: Respondents Scoring within Specified ABQ Subscale Range by Group, continued

Group Subscale Score	Emotional/ Physical Exhaustion freq.	%	Reduced Sense of Accomplishment freq.	%	Sport Devaluation freq.	%
Team Sport (n = 747)						
1 to <2	152	20.3	189	25.3	331	44.3
2 to <3	350	46.9	387	51.8	295	39.5
3 to <4	212	28.4	164	22.0	106	14.2
4 to 5	33	4.4	7	0.9	15	2.0
Conditioning Intensive (n = 1,341)						
1 to <2	218	16.3	411	30.6	645	48.1
2 to <3	567	42.3	623	46.5	479	35.7
3 to <4	436	32.5	274	20.4	172	12.8
4 to 5	120	8.9	33	2.5	45	3.4
Not Conditioning Intensive (n = 253)						
1 to <2	45	17.8	67	26.5	125	49.4
2 to <3	121	47.8	129	51.0	89	35.2
3 to <4	74	29.2	55	21.7	33	13.0
4 to 5	13	5.1	2	0.8	6	2.4

Note: Gender information missing for one case, and sport information missing for 33 cases.

Table 5.4: Number and Percentage of Respondents with all ABQ Subscale Scores Meeting a Threshold of 3 or 4 by Group

Score Threshold	Total Sample	Female	Male	Adol.	College/ Adult	Indiv. Sport	Team Sport	CI	NCI
> 3 on all subscales	112 (6.9%)	61 (9.0%)	51 (5.4%)	42 (9.9%)	70 (5.8%)	68 (8.0%)	44 (5.9%)	95 (7.1%)	17 (6.7%)
> 4 on all subscales	5 (0.3%)	2 (0.3%)	3 (0.3%)	3 (0.7%)	2 (0.2%)	4 (0.5%)	1 (0.1%)	5 (0.4%)	0 (0.0%)

Notes: From total sample of 1,627 cases. CI = conditioning intensive sport. NCI = not conditioning intensive sport.

as high burnout may or may not be of sufficient magnitude to correspond to the experience of debilitating burnout consequences. A valuable direction for future work on the ABQ would be to link burnout scores within a theoretical or clinical framework, delineating what constitutes high scores based on a state conceptualization of burnout. Developing cutoff points on the ABQ could be advanced by linking scores with consequences such as dropout, maladaptive immunological responding, and other markers (e.g., behavioral, physiological, or psychosocial) consistent with a debilitative burnout state.

It is also possible that the descriptive information presented in this chapter underestimates burnout in the larger population. Researchers using the ABQ in quantitative studies have sampled healthy athletes, unlike qualitative investigations of athlete burnout that have specifically targeted individuals deemed to have burned out from sport (e.g., Gould, Tuffey et al., 1994, 1996; Gustafsson, Kenttä, Hassmén, Lundqvist, & Durand-Bush, 2007). That is, the samples consist of actively participating athletes and therefore reflect what is referred to as the "healthy worker effect" (Schaufeli & Enzmann, 1998), where those experiencing the burnout syndrome are likely not represented. Instead, relatively healthy individuals who continue to show for work, or in this case sport, make up the participant pool. It is reasonable to expect that athletes experiencing a fully developed form of burnout would be more likely to have dropped out of sport, skipped practice sessions when the ABQ was administered, or declined study participation.

Also, it is important to acknowledge that a significant proportion of the data on the ABQ comes from swimming and rugby athletes. Further work is needed that employs the ABQ with athletes from a range of sport types and athletes representing a broad range of sport demands (e.g., physiological intensity of training, amount of time committed to training, performance stakes). As noted earlier in this manual, the developmental appropriateness of the ABQ for assessing burnout in child athletes is unknown, and careful assessment of ABQ scores will be necessary by researchers wishing to study this special population of athletes.

As a final point, it should be noted that the information provided in this chapter comes exclusively from the English language version of the ABQ completed by participants in New Zealand or the United States. Therefore, the descriptive statistics shared in this chapter, the within-network and between-network findings presented in previous chapters, and the conceptual framework underlying the ABQ may not offer a directly applicable template for interpreting ABQ scores obtained from translated versions of the measure that are administered in other cultures (Duda & Hayashi, 1998). However, findings of initial work with Chinese (Chen & Kee, in press), French (Perreault, Gaudreau, Lapointe, & Lacroix, 2007), German (Ziemainz, Abu-Omar, Raedeke, & Krause, 2004), Norwegian (Lemyre, Hall, & Roberts, 2008; Lemyre, Roberts, & Stray-Gundersen, 2007), and Swedish (Gustafsson, Kenttä, Hassmén, Lundqvist, & Durand-Bush, 2007) language versions of the ABQ have been consistent with findings that we have reported in this manual. We encourage researchers to be cognizant of cultural issues when conducting research on athlete burnout and when using the ABQ. In summary, the reader is encouraged to consider the information contained in this chapter in light of issues such as arbitrary cutoff points, the inclusion of healthy athletes in most burnout studies, the few studies using the ABQ to date, and the relatively narrow cultural reach of initial ABQ development and validation efforts.

References

American Educational Research Association. (1999). *Standards for educational and psychological testing.* Washington, DC: American Educational Research Association.

American Psychological Association. (2002). Ethical principles of psychologists and code of conduct. *American Psychologist, 57,* 1060-1073.

Beemsterboer, J., & Baum, B. H. (1984). "Burnout:" Definitions and health care management. *Social Work in Health Care, 10*(1), 97-109.

Black, J. M., & Smith, A. L. (2007). An examination of Coakley's perspective on identity, control, and burnout among adolescent athletes. *International Journal of Sport Psychology, 38,* 417-436.

Burisch, M. (1993). In search of theory: Some ruminations on the nature and etiology of burnout. In W. B. Schaufeli, C. Maslach, & T. Marek (Eds.), *Professional burnout: Recent developments in theory and research* (pp. 75-93). Washington, DC: Taylor & Francis.

Byrne, B. M. (1994). *Structural equation modeling with EQS and EQS/Windows.* London: Sage.

Byrne, B. M. (1998). *Structural equation modeling with LISREL, PRELIS, and SIMPLIS: Basic concepts, applications, and programming.* Mahwah, NJ: LEA.

Carroll, J. F. X., & White, W. L. (1982). Theory building: Integrating individual and environmental factors within an ecological framework. In W. S. Paine (Ed.), *Job stress and burnout: Research, theory, and intervention perspectives* (pp. 41-60). Beverly Hills, CA: Sage.

Chen, L. H., & Kee, Y. H. (in press). Gratitude and adolescent athletes' well-being. *Social Indicators Research.*

Cherniss, C. (1980). *Staff burnout: Job stress in the human services.* Beverly Hills, CA: Sage.

Chou, C., & Bentler, P. M. (1995). Estimates and tests in structural equation modeling. In R. H. Hoyle (Ed.), *Structural equation modeling: Concepts, issues, and applications* (pp. 37-55). Thousand Oaks, CA: Sage.

Clark, L. A. & Watson, D. (1995). Constructing validity: Basic issues in objective scale development. *Psychological Assessment, 7,* 309-319.

Coakley, J. (1992). Burnout among adolescent athletes: A personal failure or social problem? *Sociology of Sport Journal, 9,* 271-285.

Cohn, P. J. (1990). An exploratory study on sources of stress and athlete burnout in youth golf. *The Sport Psychologist, 4,* 95-106.

Cordes, C. L., & Dougherty, T. W. (1993). A review and an integration of research on job burnout. *Academy of Management Review, 18,* 621-656.

Cox, T., Tisserand, M., & Taris, T. (2005). The conceptualization and measurement of burnout: Questions and directions. *Work and Stress, 19,* 187-191.

Cox, T., Kuk, G., & Leiter, M. P. (1993). Burnout, health, work stress, and organizational healthiness. In W. B. Schaufeli, C. Maslach, & T. Marek (Eds.), *Professional burnout: Recent developments in theory and research* (pp. 177-193). Washington, DC: Taylor & Francis.

Cresswell, S. L., & Eklund, R. C. (2004). The athlete burnout syndrome: Possible early signs. *Journal of Science and Medicine in Sport, 7,* 481-487.

Cresswell, S. L., & Eklund, R. C. (2005a). Changes in athlete burnout and motivation over a 12-week league tournament. *Medicine & Science in Sports & Exercise, 37,* 1957-1966.

Cresswell, S. L., & Eklund, R. C. (2005b). Motivation and burnout among top amateur rugby players. *Medicine & Science in Sports & Exercise, 37,* 469-477.

Cresswell, S. L., & Eklund, R. C. (2005c). Motivation and burnout in professional rugby players. *Research Quarterly for Exercise and Sport, 76,* 370-376.

Cresswell, S. L., & Eklund, R. C. (2006a). Changes in athlete burnout over a thirty-week "rugby year". *Journal of Science and Medicine in Sport, 9,* 125-134.

Cresswell, S. L., & Eklund, R. C. (2006b). The convergent and discriminant validity of burnout measures in sport: A multi-trait/multi-method analysis. *Journal of Sports Sciences, 24,* 209-220.

Cresswell, S. L., & Eklund, R. C. (2006c). The nature of athlete burnout: Key characteristics and attributions. *Journal of Applied Sport Psychology, 18,* 219-239.

Cresswell, S. L., & Eklund, R. C. (2007). Athlete burnout and organizational culture: An English rugby replication. *International Journal of Sport Psychology, 38,* 365-387.

Dale, J., & Weinberg, R. (1990). Burnout in sport: A review and critique. *Journal of Applied Sport Psychology, 2,* 67-83.

Deci, E. L., & Ryan, R. M. (1985). *Intrinsic motivation and self-determination in human behavior.* New York: Plenum.

Duda, J. L., & Hayashi, C. T. (1998). Measurement issues in cross-cultural research within sport and exercise psychology. In J. L. Duda (Ed.), *Advances in sport and exercise psychology measurement* (pp. 471-483). Morgantown, WV: Fitness Information Technology.

Eades, A. M. (1990). *An investigation of burnout of intercollegiate athletes: The development of the Eades athlete burnout inventory.* Unpublished master's thesis, University of California, Berkeley.

Eklund, R. C., & Cresswell, S. L. (2007). Athlete burnout. In G. Tenenbaum & R. C. Eklund (Eds.), *Handbook of sport psychology* (3rd ed., pp. 621-641). Hoboken, NJ: Wiley.

Evans, B. K., & Fischer, D. G. (1993). The nature of burnout: A study of the three-factor model of burnout in human service and non-human service samples. *Journal of Occupational and Organizational Psychology, 66,* 29-38.

Farber, B. A. (1983). Introduction: A critical perspective on burnout. In B. A. Farber (Ed.), *Stress and burnout in the human service professions* (pp. 1-22). New York: Pergamon.

Feigley, D. A. (1984). Psychological burnout in high-level athletes. *The Physician and Sportsmedicine, 12*(10), 109-112, 115-119.

Fender, L. K. (1989). Athlete burnout: Potential for research and intervention strategies. *The Sport Psychologist, 3,* 63-71.

Freudenberger, H. J. (1974). Staff burn-out. *Journal of Social Issues, 30,* 159-165.

Freudenberger, H. J. (1983). Burnout: Contemporary issues, trends, and concerns. In B. A. Farber (Ed.), *Stress and burnout in the human service professions* (pp. 23-28). New York: Pergamon.

Freudenberger, H. J., & Richelson, G. (1980). *Burn-out: The high cost of high achievement.* Garden City, NY: Anchor.

Gaines, J., & Jermier, J. M. (1983). Emotional exhaustion in a high stress organization. *Academy of Management Journal, 26,* 567-586.

Garden, A. M. (1987). Depersonalization: A valid dimension of burnout? *Human Relations, 40,* 545-560.

Garden, A. M. (1989). Burnout: The effect of psychological type on research findings. *Journal of Occupational Psychology, 62,* 223-234.

Golembiewski, R. T., Munzenrider, R., & Carter, D. (1983). Phases of progressive burnout and their work site covariants: Critical issues in OD research and praxis. *Journal of Applied Behavioral Science, 19,* 461-481.

Goodger, K., Gorely, T., Lavallee, D., & Harwood, C. (2007). Burnout in sport: A systematic review. *The Sport Psychologist, 21,* 127-151.

Goodger, K., Wolfenden, L., & Lavallee, D. (2007). Symptoms and consequences associated with three dimensions of burnout in junior tennis players. *International Journal of Sport Psychology, 38,* 342-364.

Gould, D. (1993). Intensive sport participation and the prepubescent athlete: Competitive stress and burnout. In B. R. Cahill & A. J. Pearl (Eds.), *Intensive participation in children's sport* (pp. 19-38). Champaign, IL: Human Kinetics.

Gould, D. (1996). Personal motivation gone awry: Burnout in competitive athletes. *Quest, 48,* 275-289.

Gould, D., Tuffey, S., Udry, E., & Loehr, J. (1994). *Burnout in competitive junior tennis players* (a United States Tennis Association sports science grant final report). Greensboro, NC: University of North Carolina Department of Exercise and Sport Science.

Gould, D., Tuffey, S., Udry, E., & Loehr, J. (1996). Burnout in competitive junior tennis players: II. Qualitative analysis. *The Sport Psychologist, 10,* 342-366.

Gould, D., Udry, E., Tuffey, S., & Loehr, J. (1996). Burnout in competitive junior tennis players: I. A quantitative psychological assessment. *The Sport Psychologist, 10,* 322-340.

Gustafsson, H., Hassmén, P., Kenttä, G., & Johansson, M. (in press). A qualitative analysis of burnout in elite Swedish athletes. *Psychology of Sport and Exercise.*

Gustafsson, H., Kenttä, G., Hassmén, P., & Lundqvist, C. (2007). Prevalence of burnout in competitive adolescent athletes. *The Sport Psychologist, 21,* 21-37.

Gustafsson, H., Kenttä, G., Hassmén, P., Lundqvist, C., & Durand-Bush, N. (2007). The process of burnout: A multiple case study of three elite endurance athletes. *International Journal of Sport Psychology, 38,* 388-416.

Halbesleben, J. R. B., & Buckley, M. R. (2004). Burnout in organizational life. *Journal of Management, 30,* 859-879.

Halbesleben, J. R. B., & Demerouti, E. (2005). The construct validity of an alternative measure of burnout: Investigating the English translation of the Oldenburg Burnout Inventory. *Work and Stress, 19,* 208-220.

Hallsten, L. (1993). Burning out: A framework. In W. B. Schaufeli, C. Maslach, & T. Marek (Eds.), *Professional burnout: Recent developments in theory and research* (pp. 95-113). Washington, DC: Taylor & Francis.

Henschen, K. P. (1990). Prevention and treatment of athletic staleness and burnout. *Sports Science Periodical on Research and Technology in Sport, 10*(5), 1-8.

Hu, L., & Bentler, P. M. (1998). Fit indices in covariance structure modeling: Sensitivity to underparameterized model misspecification. *Psychological Methods, 3,* 424-453.

Hu, L., & Bentler, P. M. (1999). Cutoff criteria for fit indexes in covariance structure analysis: Conventional criteria versus new alternatives. *Structural Equation Modeling, 6*, 1-55.

Jackson, S. E., Schwab, R. L., & Schuler, R. S. (1986). Toward an understanding of the burnout phenomenon. *Journal of Applied Psychology, 71*, 630-640.

Kahill, S. A. (1988). Symptoms of professional burnout: A review of the empirical evidence. *Canadian Psychology, 29*, 284-297.

Kalliath, T. J., O'Driscoll, M. P., Gillespie, D. F., & Bluedorn, A. C. (2000). A test of the Maslach Burnout Inventory in three samples of healthcare professionals. *Work and Stress, 14*, 35-50.

Kleiber, D., & Enzmann, D. (1990). *Burnout: 15 years of research: An international bibliography.* Göttingen: Hogrefe.

Koeske, G. F., & Koeske, R. D. (1989). Construct validity of the Maslach Burnout Inventory: A critical review and reconceptualization. *Journal of Applied Behavioral Science, 25*, 131-144.

Koeske, G. F., & Koeske, R. D. (1993). A preliminary test of a stress-strain-outcome model for reconceptualizing the burnout phenomenon. *Journal of Social Service Research, 17*(3/4), 107-135.

Kristensen, T. S., Borritz, M., Villadsen, E., & Christensen, K. B. (2005). The Copenhagen Burnout Inventory: A new tool for the assessment of burnout. *Work and Stress, 19*, 192-207.

Lazarus, R. S. (1990). Theory-based stress measurement. *Psychological Inquiry, 1*, 3-13.

Lee, R. T., & Ashforth, B. E. (1993). A longitudinal study of burnout among supervisors and managers: Comparisons between Leiter and Maslach (1988) and Golembiewski et al. (1986) models. *Organizational Behavior and Human Decision Processes, 54*, 369-398.

Leiter, M. P. (1991). Coping patterns as predictors of burnout: The function of control and escapist coping patterns. *Journal of Organizational Behavior, 12*, 123-144.

Leiter, M. P. (1992). Burnout as a crisis in self-efficacy: Conceptual and practical implications. *Work and Stress, 6*, 107-115.

Leiter, M. P. (1993). Burnout as a developmental process: Consideration of models. In W. B. Schaufeli, C. Maslach, & T. Marek (Eds.), *Professional burnout: Recent developments in theory and research* (pp. 237-250). Washington, DC: Taylor & Francis.

Leiter, M. P., & Maslach, C. (1988). The impact of interpersonal environment on burnout and organizational commitment. *Journal of Organizational Behavior, 9*, 297-308.

Leiter, M. P., & Schaufeli, W. B. (1996). Consistency of the burnout construct across occupations. *Anxiety, Stress, & Coping, 9*, 229-243.

Lemyre, P.-N., Hall, H. K., & Roberts, G. C. (2008). A social cognitive approach to burnout in elite athletes. *Scandinavian Journal of Medicine & Science in Sports, 18*, 221-234.

Lemyre, P.-N., Roberts, G. C., & Stray-Gundersen, J. (2007). Motivation, overtraining, and burnout: Can self-determined motivation predict overtraining and burnout in elite athletes? *European Journal of Sport Science, 7*, 115-126.

Lemyre, P.-N., Treasure, D. C., & Roberts, G. C. (2006). Influence of variability in motivation and affect on elite athlete burnout susceptibility. *Journal of Sport & Exercise Psychology, 28*, 32-48.

Lonsdale, C. (2005). *Burnout out or burning desire? Investigating athlete burnout and engagement in elite New Zealand athletes.* Unpublished doctoral dissertation, University of Otago, New Zealand.

Lonsdale, C., Hodge, K., & Jackson, S. A. (2007). Athlete engagement: II. Development and initial validation of the Athlete Engagement Questionnaire. *International Journal of Sport Psychology, 38*, 471-492.

Lonsdale, C., Hodge, K., & Raedeke, T. D. (2007). Athlete engagement: I. A qualitative investigation of relevance and dimensions. *International Journal of Sport Psychology, 38*, 451-470.

Lonsdale, C., Hodge, K., & Rose, E. A. (2006). Pixels vs. paper: Comparing online and traditional survey methods in sport psychology. *Journal of Sport & Exercise Psychology, 28*, 100-108.

MacNeil, D. H. (1981). The relationship of occupational stress to burnout. In J. W. Jones (Ed.), *The burnout syndrome: Current research, theory, and interventions* (pp. 68-88). Park Ridge, IL: London House.

Marcia, J. E. (1994). The empirical study of ego identity. In H. A. Bosma, T. L. G. Graafsma, H. D. Grotevant, & D. J. de Levita (Eds.), *Identity and development: An interdisciplinary approach* (pp. 67-80). Thousand Oaks, CA: Sage.

Marcia, J. E., Waterman, A. S., Matteson, D. R., Archer, S. L., & Orlofsky, J. L. (1993). *Ego identity: A handbook for psychosocial research.* New York: Springer-Verlag.

Marsh, H. W. (1998). Foreword. In J. L. Duda (Ed.), *Advances in sport and exercise psychology measurement* (pp. xv-xix). Morgantown, WV: Fitness Information Technology.

Marsh, H. W., Hau, K-T., & Wen, Z. (2004). In search of golden rules: Comment on hypothesis-testing approaches to setting cutoff values for fit indexes and dangers in overgeneralizing Hu and Bentler's (1999) findings. *Structural Equation Modeling, 11*, 320-341.

Maslach, C. (1976). Burned-Out. *Human Behavior, 5*, 16-22.

Maslach, C. (1982). Understanding burnout: Definitional issues in analyzing a complex phenomenon. In W. S. Paine (Ed.), *Job stress and burnout: Research, theory, and intervention perspectives* (pp. 29-40). Beverly Hills, CA: Sage.

Maslach, C. (1993). Burnout: A multidimensional perspective. In W. B. Schaufeli, C. Maslach, & T. Marek (Eds.), *Professional burnout: Recent developments in theory and research* (pp. 19-32). Washington, DC: Taylor & Francis.

Maslach, C., & Goldberg, J. (1998). Prevention of burnout: New perspectives. *Applied and Preventive Psychology, 7*, 63-74.

Maslach, C., & Jackson, S. E. (1981). The measurement of experienced burnout. *Journal of Occupational Behaviour, 2*, 99-113.

Maslach, C., & Jackson, S. E. (1984). Burnout in organizational settings. In S. Oskamp (Ed.), *Applied social psychology annual: Applications in organizational settings* (Vol. 5, pp. 133-153). Beverly Hills, CA: Sage.

Maslach, C., Jackson, S. E., & Leiter, M. P. (1996). *Maslach burnout inventory manual* (3rd ed.). Palo Alto, CA: Consulting Psychologists Press.

Maslach, C., & Schaufeli, W. B. (1993). Historical and conceptual development of burnout. In W. B. Schaufeli, C. Maslach, & T. Marek (Eds.), *Professional burnout: Recent developments in theory and research* (pp. 1-16). Washington, DC: Taylor & Francis.

Maslach, C., Schaufeli, W. B., & Leiter, M. P. (2001). Job burnout. *Annual Review of Psychology, 52*, 397-422.

Messick, S. (1995). Validity of psychological assessment: Validation of inferences from persons' responses and performances as scientific inquiry into score meaning. *American Psychologist, 50*, 741-749.

Miller, K., & Kobelski, P. (1982). *Burnout: A multidisciplinary bibliography.* Monticello, IL: Vance Bibliographies.

Morrow, L. (1981). The burnout of almost everyone. *Time, 118*(12), 84.

Pelletier, L. G., Fortier, M. S., Vallerand, R. J., Tuson, K. M., Brière, N. M., & Blais, M. R. (1995). Toward a new measure of intrinsic motivation, extrinsic motivation, and amotivation in sports: The Sport Motivation Scale (SMS). *Journal of Sport & Exercise Psychology, 17*, 35-53.

Perlman, B., & Hartman, E. A. (1982). Burnout: Summary and future research. *Human Relations, 35*, 283-305.

Perreault, S., Gaudreau, P., Lapointe, M-C., & Lacroix, C. (2007). Does it take three to tango? Psychological need satisfaction and athlete burnout. *International Journal of Sport Psychology, 38*, 437-450.

Pick, D., & Leiter, M. P. (1991). Nurses' perceptions of the nature and causes of burnout: A comparison of self-reports and standardized measures. *Canadian Journal of Nursing Research, 23*(3), 33-48.

Pines, A. M. (1993). Burnout: An existential perspective. In W. B. Schaufeli, C. Maslach, & T. Marek (Eds.), *Professional burnout: Recent developments in theory and research* (pp. 33-51). Washington, DC: Taylor & Francis.

Pines, A. M., & Aronson, E. (1988). *Career burnout: Causes and cures.* New York: Free Press.

Price, M. S., & Weiss, M. R. (2000). Relationships among coach burnout, coach behaviors, and athletes' psychological responses. *The Sport Psychologist, 14*, 391-409.

Raedeke, T. D. (1995). *Is athlete burnout more than just stress? A sport commitment perspective.* Unpublished doctoral dissertation, University of Oregon, Eugene.

Raedeke, T. D. (1997). Is athlete burnout more than just stress? A sport commitment perspective. *Journal of Sport & Exercise Psychology, 19*, 396-417.

Raedeke, T. D., Lunney, K., & Venables, K. (2002). Understanding athlete burnout: Coach perspectives. *Journal of Sport Behavior, 25*, 181-206.

Raedeke, T. D., & Smith, A. L. (2001). Development and preliminary validation of an athlete burnout measure. *Journal of Sport & Exercise Psychology, 23*, 281-306.

Raedeke, T. D., & Smith, A. L. (2004). Coping resources and athletic burnout: An examination of stress mediated and moderation hypotheses. *Journal of Sport & Exercise Psychology, 26*, 525-541.

Rafferty, A. P., Lemkau, J. P., Purdy, R. R., & Rudisill, J. R. (1986). Validity of the Maslach Burnout Inventory for family practice physicians. *Journal of Clinical Psychology, 42*, 488-492.

Rotella, R. J., Hanson, T., & Coop, R. H. (1991). Burnout in youth sports. *Elementary School Journal, 91*, 421-428.

Rowe, D. A., & Mahar, M. T. (2006). Validity. In T. M. Wood & W. Zhu (Eds.), *Measurement theory and practice in kinesiology* (pp. 9-26). Champaign, IL: Human Kinetics.

Schaufeli, W. B., Bakker, A. B., Hoogduin, K., Schaap, C., & Kladler, A. (2001). On the clinical validity of the Maslach Burnout Inventory and the Burnout Measure. *Psychology and Health, 16*, 565-582.

Schaufeli, W., & Enzmann, D. (1998). *The burnout companion to study and practice: A critical analysis.* London: Taylor & Francis.

Schaufeli, W. B., Maslach, C., & Marek, T. (1993). *Professional burnout: Recent developments in theory and research.* Washington, DC: Taylor & Francis.

Schaufeli, W. B., & Taris, T. W. (2005). The conceptualization and measurement of burnout: Common ground and worlds apart. *Work and Stress, 19*, 256-262.

Schmidt, G. W., & Stein, G. L. (1991). Sport commitment: A model integrating enjoyment, dropout, and burnout. *Journal of Sport & Exercise Psychology, 13*, 254-265.

Schutte, N., Toppinen, S., Kalimo, R., & Schaufeli, W. (2000). The factorial validity of the Maslach Burnout Inventory-General Survey (MBI-GS) across occupational groups and nations. *Journal of Occupational and Organizational Psychology, 73*, 53-66.

Shirom, A. (1989). Burnout in work organizations. In C. L. Cooper & I. Robertson (Eds.), *International review of industrial and organizational psychology* (pp. 25-48). Chichester, England: Wiley.

Shirom, A. (2005). Reflections on the study of burnout. *Work and Stress, 19*, 263-207.

Silva, J. M. (1990). An analysis of the training stress syndrome in competitive athletics. *Journal of Applied Sport Psychology, 2*, 5-20.

Smith, A. L., Lemyre, P.-N., & Raedeke, T. D. (2007). Advances in athlete burnout research. *International Journal of Sport Psychology, 38*, 337-341.

Smith, R. E. (1986). Toward a cognitive-affective model of athletic burnout. *Journal of Sport Psychology, 8*, 36-50.

Starrin, B., Larsson, G., & Styrborn, S. (1990). A review and critique of psychological approaches to the burn-out phenomenon. *Scandinavian Journal of Caring Sciences, 4*, 83-91.

Taris, T. W., Le Blanc, P. M., Schaufeli, W. B., & Schreurs, P. J. G. (2005). Are there casual relationships between the dimensions of the Maslach Burnout Inventory? A review of two longitudinal tests. *Work and Stress, 19*, 238-255.

Wallace, J. E., & Brinkerhoff, M. B. (1991). The measurement of burnout revisited. *Journal of Social Service Research, 14*(1/2), 85-111.

Weinberg, R. (1990). Training stress: A need for more research. *Journal of Applied Sport Psychology, 2*, 1-4.

Wiggins, M. S., Cremades, J. G., Lai, C., Lee, J., & Erdmann, J. B. (2006). Multidimensional comparison of anxiety direction and burnout over time. *Perceptual and Motor Skills, 102*, 788-790.

Yukelson, D. (1990). Psychological burnout in sport participants. *Sports Medicine Digest, 12*(5), 4.

Ziemainz, H., Abu-Omar, K., Raedeke, T., & Krause, K. (2004). Burnout im Sport: Zur Prävalenz von Burnout aus bedingungsbezogener Perspektive. *Leistungssport, 34*, 12-17.

Zumbo, B. D. (2005). Structural equation modeling and test validation. In B. Everitt & D. C. Howell (Eds.), *Encyclopedia of statistics in behavioral science* (pp. 1951-1958). Chichester, UK: Wiley.

Appendix A:
The Athlete Burnout Questionnaire

Please read each statement carefully and decide if you ever feel this way about your current sport participation. Your current sport participation includes all the training you have completed during this season. Please indicate how often you have had this feeling or thought this season by circling a number 1 to 5, where 1 means "I almost never feel this way" and 5 means "I feel that way most of the time." There are no right or wrong answers, so please answer each question as honestly as you can. Please make sure you answer all items. If you have any questions, feel free to ask.

How often do you feel this way?	Almost Never	Rarely	Some- times	Frequently	Almost Always
1. I'm accomplishing many worthwhile things in [*sport*]	1	2	3	4	5
2. I feel so tired from my training that I have trouble finding energy to do other things	1	2	3	4	5
3. The effort I spend in [*sport*] would be better spent doing other things	1	2	3	4	5
4. I feel overly tired from my [*sport*] participation	1	2	3	4	5
5. I am not achieving much in [*sport*]	1	2	3	4	5
6. I don't care as much about my [*sport*] performance as I used to	1	2	3	4	5
7. I am not performing up to my ability in [*sport*]	1	2	3	4	5
8. I feel "wiped out" from [*sport*]	1	2	3	4	5
9. I'm not into [*sport*] like I used to be	1	2	3	4	5
10. I feel physically worn out from [*sport*]	1	2	3	4	5
11. I feel less concerned about being successful in [*sport*] than I used to	1	2	3	4	5
12. I am exhausted by the mental and physical demands of [*sport*]	1	2	3	4	5
13. It seems that no matter what I do, I don't perform as well as I should	1	2	3	4	5
14. I feel successful at [*sport*]	1	2	3	4	5
15. I have negative feelings toward [*sport*]	1	2	3	4	5

Note: The specific sport of the respondent is inserted where [sport] appears above. For example, in a swimming-specific study item one would read "I'm accomplishing many worthwhile things in swimming".

Appendix B: Scoring of the Athlete Burnout Questionnaire

Emotional/Physical Exhaustion

        Item 2
        Item 4
        Item 8
        Item 10
+   Item 12

Sum of Item Scores ÷ 5 = *Emotional/Physical Exhaustion Subscale Score*

Reduced Sense of Accomplishment

        Item 1 → reverse scored (5, 4, 3, 2, 1)
        Item 5
        Item 7
        Item 13
+   Item 14 → reverse scored (5, 4, 3, 2, 1)

Sum of Item Scores ÷ 5 = *Reduced Sense of Accomplishment Subscale Score*

Sport Devaluation

        Item 3
        Item 6
        Item 9
        Item 11
+   Item 15

Sum of Item Scores ÷ 5 = *Sport Devaluation Subscale Score*

About the Authors

Al Smith (left) and Tom Raedeke (right) – October, 1999

Thomas D. Raedeke and **Alan L. Smith** met in 1993 at the University of Oregon, where they shared an office as graduate students in the Department of Exercise and Movement Science. Their mutual interests in motivational processes in sport led to their later collaboration on the development of the Athlete Burnout Questionnaire (ABQ), which built from Raedeke's doctoral dissertation research on commitment and burnout in adolescent swimmers. That work received the 1995 National Association for Sport and Physical Education (NASPE) Sport Psychology Academy and 1996 Association for the Advancement of Applied Sport Psychology dissertation awards. Raedeke and Smith's collaboration on athlete burnout research and the development of the ABQ began in their early assistant professor years. Currently, they are associate professors at East Carolina University and Purdue University, respectively, and continue their collaborative activity. Most recently, they co-edited a special issue of the *International Journal of Sport Psychology* on athlete burnout (Smith, Lemyre, & Raedeke, 2007). Raedeke and Smith both have served as chair of the NASPE Sport and Exercise Psychology Academy, serve on the editorial board of the *Journal of Applied Sport Psychology*, and are certified consultants through the Association for Applied Sport Psychology (AASP). Beyond their shared professional backgrounds, Raedeke is currently chair of the AASP Health and Exercise Psychology committee and recently co-authored a text titled *Sport Psychology for Coaches*. His work on burnout stems from a broader interest in affective experiences and motivational processes as they relate to promoting positive sport and exercise experiences that foster continued involvement and psychological well-being. Smith is an associate editor of the *Journal of Sport & Exercise Psychology* and a consulting editor of *Child Development*. He is widely recognized for his work on peer relationships in sport and physical activity contexts and, in addition to co-developing the ABQ, co-developed the Sport Friendship Quality Scale (Weiss & Smith, 1999, 2002).